PREACHING FROM THE BIBLE

PREACHING
FROM
THE BIBLE

ANDREW W. BLACKWOOD
Professor of Homiletics
THE THEOLOGICAL SEMINARY
Princeton, New Jersey

BAKER BOOK HOUSE
Grand Rapids, Michigan

Copyright © 1941 by Whitmore & Stone
Copyright renewal 1969 by Carolyn P. Blackwood
Reprinted 1974 by Baker Book House
with the permission of
Abingdon Press

ISBN: 0-8010-0619-8

PHOTOLITHOPRINTED BY CUSHING - MALLOY, INC.
ANN ARBOR, MICHIGAN, UNITED STATES OF AMERICA
1974

DEDICATED
TO
THE MOTHER
OF
THE YOUNG MINISTER

FOREWORD

"Where can we find a minister who knows how to preach from the Bible?" This question comes from the chairman of a committee in quest of a pastor. "Our people loved our former minister, but they soon grew weary of his sermons. Every year, after the first few weeks in the fall, he seemed to be all preached out." Doubtless such laymen are unduly critical. Perhaps they have kept their pastor so busy about many things that they have left him little time to think about the Bible or the art of preaching. The fact remains that many of our strongest laymen would relish at least one inspiring biblical message every Lord's Day. Surely they have a right to insist that their minister should know how to prepare and deliver such a strong, gripping sermon.

"Where can I get a book which will tell me how to prepare a sermon from the Bible?" This question comes from a parish minister. Last summer he attended a Bible conference where he eagerly drank in all that the lecturers could draw from the wells of salvation. When he came home he determined that he too would do some of this drawing. But, alas, he has found that the well is deep, and that he has nothing to draw with. He wishes that he could secure a leave of absence and spend a year in postgraduate work, that he might learn how to preach from the Bible. He does not yet realize that the best classroom in biblical homiletics is the study of the parish minister.

"Where can I secure a textbook about preaching from the Bible?" This question comes from a professor in a seminary which offers two elective courses in this difficult field. The teacher is familiar with the few available books about expository preaching,[1] but he is conscious of the need for something additional. He wants a book filled with concrete cases, which will show the student how he can preach from the Bible, as well as what he should preach. Of course there should be a certain amount of theory, but there should be much more that is practical, in a form which the student can take into the "laboratory" where he is learning how to handle his homiletical tools. With few exceptions, the young men in our theological seminaries wish that they could learn how to preach from the Bible.

These three questions indicate three practical reasons for the present book. It has grown out of long, happy years in pastorates of various sorts, and other long, happy years as a teacher of young ministers. In preparing each chapter the main dependence has been upon personal study of the Bible, and upon careful study of biblical sermons by master preachers. Almost without exception, every theory in the book has come to me from a study of preaching throughout the history of the Church, beginning with the Old Testament prophets; and every practical proposal has grown out of some present-day pastor's experience. One after another, these theories and practical proposals have gone through the students' "laboratory" here at the Seminary. Better still, these theories and practical proposals have stood the acid test of use in hundreds of local parishes, many of which are small and exacting.

---

[1] E.g., *How to Prepare an Expository Sermon,* by H. E. Knott, Standard Publishing Co., Cincinnati, 1930; *The Use of the Bible in Preaching,* by Carl S. Patton, Willett, Clark, Chicago, 1936.

FOREWORD

For indirect help in preparing the book I am grateful to the students, past and present, whose diligent labors have taught me much about preaching from the Bible; to our librarian and his assistants, whose unfailing helpfulness makes working with books a pleasure; to the publishers, whose many kindnesses include the report that their patrons have been asking for a book on this subject; and to various pastors, whose published sermons and lists of special series have provided me with abundance of practical material.

Above all am I grateful to the Heavenly Father for the gift of the Book, and for the promise of the Holy Spirit. The Bible should ever be our supreme book about preaching, and the Holy Spirit should be our Teacher.

ANDREW W. BLACKWOOD.

The Theological Seminary
Princeton, New Jersey.

CONTENTS

CONTENTS

CHAPTER I

THE PREACHER'S EXAMPLES

THE theory which undergirds this book is that the Bible should be the basis of the minister's pulpit work. In order to make this theory fairly clear and luminous, let us look at certain master preachers of yesterday and today. These men have owed much of their popular effectiveness, under God, to the fact that they have been skillful interpreters of the Scriptures. The reason for turning to them now is to set up ideals for the present-day minister who wishes to preach more largely from the Bible.

In other words, let us use the "case method." The modern way to study preaching, or any other art which is practical, is to single out cases worthy of note, and then observe them one by one. Unfortunately, we shall have time only to glance at each of our chosen examples. We shall consider him solely as an object lesson of how to use the Bible from the pulpit in meeting the needs of men and women. Of course every one of these homiletical heroes has been notable for other reasons which we shall not consider. The subject before us, preaching from the Bible, is so vast and so varied that we shall have time for nothing else, however worthy.

Meanwhile there are other theories about preaching, as there are other sorts of useful sermons. Throughout the history of the Church there have been master preachers who seem not to have relied chiefly upon the Scriptures as the basis of their pulpit work. For light upon such other ways of preaching one need only turn to well-known books about homiletics.[1] Surely there is no desire to find fault with any sort of sermon which exalts Jesus Christ as Saviour and King. In all such matters every local minister has to work out his own salvation. In doing so he may well think about certain master preachers.

NEW TESTAMENT MASTERS

In any account of Christian preaching the obvious place to begin is with our Lord. He is vastly more than our object lesson. He is our ideal Preacher. By his example he shows us how to meet all sorts of human needs. In what seems to have been his first sermon, at the synagogue in Nazareth, his home town, he took as the basis of his message certain golden words from Isaiah.[2] From that time on, whether our Lord was preaching in the synagogue or in the open, he used the Old Testament as the warp of his spoken word. For example, on the road to Emmaus, in one of his final messages before the Ascension, "he expounded unto them in all the scriptures the things concerning himself." [3]

This same biblical quality appears in the preaching of the apostles. Sometimes, as with Stephen when he was about to be stoned, the exposition was extensive.[4] Once in a long while, perhaps once in a lifetime, at a service of farewell, there may be a call for such a comprehensive discourse. As a rule it is better for the parish minister to follow the example of Philip when he opened up the Scriptures. Instead of trying to

---

[1] E.g., *The Christian Preacher,* by Alfred E. Garvie, Scribner, 1921.
[2] Isa. 61:1, 2a; Luke 4:18, 19.
[3] Luke 24:25-27. In the Greek study the verb "expounded."
[4] Acts 7.

16

explain all about the Old Testament, Philip kept to his one passage in Isaiah. The record in the Book of Acts[5] suggests some of the principles which should govern all our preaching from the Bible.

The popular interpreter of the Scriptures begins with something of interest to his hearer. This is what the modern writer terms a psychological approach. Such a way of seeking entrance to the City of Mansoul is by no means new. When our Lord was talking with the woman who had come to draw water from the community well, he began to speak about water. When Philip addressed the stranger who was reading from the Bible, the opening words had to do with the Book: "Understandest thou what thou readest?" The reply is one that the man in the pew wishes to make whenever the man in the pulpit asks if he understands the Scriptures: "How can I except some one shall guide me?"

The minister, therefore, is the layman's guide into the understanding of the Bible. "Philip opened his mouth and beginning from the same scripture preached unto him Jesus." What if the interpreter had tried to explain diverse critical theories about Deutero-Isaiah, or Trito-Isaiah, and about the Servant of the Lord? Of course every educated minister knows about such things, but he keeps quiet about them when he is trying to explain from the pulpit what the layman needs to know in order to begin doing the will of God. What the layman needs to know, most of all, is what the Ethiopian treasurer learned—the truth as it is in Jesus Christ.

Herein lies the secret of the Christian radiance which the

---

[5] Acts 8:26-40; Isa. 53:7, 8. In Acts 8:31 the verb "guide" is the same as in John 16:13a, where the Holy Spirit is the Guide.

present-day Church seems largely to have lost. In the Apostolic Church that radiance began to glow after the Resurrection of our Lord. "Did not our hearts burn within us while he talked with us by the way, and while he opened to us the scriptures?" [6] In the Apostolic Church the preaching was in the spirit of prayer. Both prayer and preaching led to the winning of souls. From that time to this, wherever the life and work of pastor and people have been notable for the use of the Bible, the spirit of prayer, and the practice of personal evangelism, there has been no local problem about "the lost radiance of the Christian Church."

EARLY CHURCH FATHERS

This same spirit of biblical Christianity carried over into the Early Church. Since we have time to consider only a few examples, let us take a long leap in time and look at two master preachers near the close of the fourth century. The most eloquent preacher in the Early Church was Chrysostom (347-407). As an orator with a passion for righteousness Chrysostom had unsurpassed powers of appeal to the imagination and the conscience of the man in the street, as well as the queen on her throne. Even in translation,[7] his ethical sermons are worthy of study as models of preaching style. His best-known sermons are the twenty *Homilies on the Statues.* Valuable, also, are his hundred and eighty *Homilies on Saint Matthew.* The life and work of Chrysostom will repay careful study on the part of any minister.

We have in Chrysostom two qualities which in their combi-

---

[6] Luke 24:32.
[7] See *Nicene and Post-Nicene Fathers,* ed. by Philip Schaff, Scribner, 1903, Vol. XI.

nation make him unique: he is a man of the Word and a man of the world. . . . . Chrysostom himself is saturated with the Scriptures, and is determined that his audience shall base their lives upon the principles of the Holy Word. . . . . He thus made himself the popular interpreter of the Christian documents, always endeavoring to get at the exact sense, and to preach the truth honestly and fearlessly.

The homilies of Chrysostom are not the expositions of a lecturer, but what is very different, the expositions of a preacher. There is a very wide contrast between the one who is only a teacher, a lecturer, an essayist, and the one who is a preacher and a prophet. It has always seemed to me that there is much force in the modern appeal for expository preaching. I only insist that it must be preaching. The classroom is one place; the pulpit is another.[8]

Chrysostom's contemporary, Augustine (354-430), Bishop of Hippo, was another gifted preacher. He has left us 394 sermons, among which the best known are his *Homilies on Saint John.* Even more worthy of note than his sermons are his other writings, especially three: *The Confessions, The City of God,* and his treatise on homiletics. In this last book, which is second to none in its field, Augustine stresses both biblical substance and literary form. In his day the two were supposed to be inseparable. Something of his mastery over words appears in the following excerpts from his treatise on preaching.

"Our teacher is necessarily the spokesman of great subjects. . . . . When God is being praised, either for himself or his works, what a glory of beautiful and splendid language wells forth for one who can go to the very lengths of praise of him whom no one can praise, but whom no one fails to praise

---

[8] *The Romance of Preaching,* by C. Silvester Horne, Revell, 1914. This is one of the most eloquent series of Yale Lectures.

in one way or another." However, "A thing is not well said unless it be truthfully said; nor should the teacher serve words, but words the teacher." All the while, says Augustine, the aim of the preacher should be to please and instruct, in order to persuade. "The Word of God belongs to those who obey it." [9]

After the days of Chrysostom and Augustine, Christian preaching began to decline. One reason was that it largely ceased to be biblical. Another reason was that the biblical preaching became increasingly allegorical; that is, unreal and fantastic. Such neglect or abuse of the Bible in preaching did much to bring about the Reformation. That mighty movement was in part an endeavor to put the Bible back into the preaching as well as the doctrine and the ethics of the Christian Church. Of course the real desire was to bring the Church and the individual soul face to face with the Living Christ as he makes himself known in the Scriptures. In so far as we Protestants are true to the ideals of the Reformation we are committed to a ministry which is biblical, at least in spirit. Fortunately, such emphasis upon the Bible as the basis of preaching has appeared among the leading divines in almost every branch of the Christian Church.

LITURGICAL CHURCH LEADERS

The Lutheran Church, for example, owes her existence, under God, to a mighty preacher. Martin Luther (1483-1546) regarded the sermon as the most important part of public worship, with the exception of the Lord's Supper. As the basis of the sermon he used a pericope; that is, one of

---

[9] *De doctrina christiana,* IV, 39, 61, 62.

the lessons appointed by the church. Much of his pulpit work was directly expository. In his *Table Talk*,[10] where he lists nine essentials of good preaching, the first is "the ability to teach systematically." From that day to this, whenever the Lutheran Church in any land has been true to the ideals of her founder, she has been a teaching church. What she teaches, largely through the local pastor, is the Bible.

The practical philosophy of Luther as a preacher shines out from the following:

When I was young, and especially before I became acquainted with theology, I dealt largely in allegories and tropes and a quantity of idle craft; but now I have let all that slip, and my best craft is to give the Scripture, with its clear meaning; for the plain meaning is learning and life. . . . . No one understands the Scriptures unless he be acquainted with the Cross.

Since this is true, Martin Niemöller, erstwhile pastor at Berlin, surely ought to understand the Scriptures. So should untold hosts of suffering saints in Europe, for their faith has been tested in the burning fiery furnace.

In the Established Church of England, likewise, the tradition calls for biblical preaching. Fortunately, the lessons in the Prayer Book lend themselves admirably to sermonic uses. Greatest of all the British preachers was probably Frederick W. Robertson (1816-53). He is often known as "the preacher's preacher." Like other masters of our art, he did not begin to be widely known until after he had finished his brief earthly career. Now the printed sermons of F. W. Robertson are on the shelves of almost every thoughtful minister. These

---

[10] Translated and edited by Wm. Hazlitt, London, 1895, p. 182.

sermons are notable examples of the textual method. Through them Robertson has profoundly influenced the teaching of homiletics, as well as the popular preaching of our day. On the shelf with his sermons there should likewise stand his expository lectures on First and Second Corinthians, and on Genesis; as well as his biography, which is one of the best works of its kind.[11]

As a teaching minister Robertson depended largely on the structure of the sermon. He says:

Detached facts are practically valueless. All public speakers know the value of method. . . . . It simply depends upon correct arrangement. . . . . Upon the correctness of the arrangement all depends. Sometimes a man will find that his divisions have been artificial, and not natural. A thought is put down under a certain head, but there is no reason why it had not been in an earlier division. It belongs to both—a sure proof that the division has been false and confused. Then, in speaking, perhaps it suggests itself under the first head; and when he comes to the one where it was to have been there is a gap, and he stumbles and blunders.[12]

In choosing his passage and in preparing his sermon Robertson depended chiefly upon the principle of contrast. Partly for this reason a typical Robertsonian sermon has only two main parts. As a rule he puts the positive before the negative, but in his sermon about the Parable of the Sower [13] he wisely follows his passage. He is speaking primarily to the young members of his confirmation class, who are soon to take their first communion. At other times his sermons show how to

---

[11] *The Life and Letters of Fred. W. Robertson,* by Stopford A. Brooke, 2 vols., London, 1873-75.

[12] *Op. cit.,* II, 126.

[13] *Sermons Preached at Brighton,* 5 vols., London, 1888, I, 16-35 (Matt. 13:1-9, 18-23).

JAMES H. CONNER

use the Bible in meeting the broader needs of one's own day. As a study of the following outline will show, his main ideas come out of the passage, but still they have to do with the practical needs of the hearer. These are the points which stand out strongly:

I The Causes of Failure (in hearing the Word)
    A Want of spiritual perception (wayside soil)
    B Want of depth in character (stony soil)
    C Presence of dissipating influences (thorny soil)
II The Permanence of Religious Impressions
    A Earnestness ("an honest and good heart")
    B Meditation (they "keep" the Word)
    C Patience ("bring forth fruit with patience")

If Robertson with his love of order and balance is the favorite preacher of many who teach homiletics, Phillips Brooks (1835-93), the beloved pastor of Trinity Episcopal Church, Boston, is a close second. His conception of his high calling appears best in his famous *Lectures on Preaching,* delivered at Yale.[14] He is pleading for "largeness of movement, the great utterance of great truths, the great enforcement of great duties, as distinct from the minute, and subtle, and ingenious treatment of little topics, side issues of the soul's life, bits of anatomy, the bric-a-brac of theology."

He is pleading, also, for the practical use of the Bible:

The preaching which is wholly exposition men are apt to find dull and pointless. It is heat lightning that quivers over many topics but strikes nowhere. The preaching which is the discussion of a topic may be interesting, but it grows unsatisfactory because it does not fasten itself to the authority

[14] E. P. Dutton and Co., New York, 1877, pp. 17, 130.

of Scripture. It tempts the preacher's genius and invention, but is apt to send people away with a feeling that they have heard him more than they have heard God. . . . . It is better to start by feeling that every sermon must have a solid rest on Scripture, and the pointedness which comes of a clear subject.

Another example of practical preaching is John Wesley (1703-91), whom we may consider here because he marks the transition from the liturgical to the non-liturgical. In common with those who labored with him in transforming the religious and social life of Britain, John Wesley looked upon the Bible as the Word of God; and he found in it the unfailing source of soul-food for new-born congregations. Among his published works [15] are a hundred and forty of his sermons, most of which are biblical in substance rather than form. The messages most nearly expository are the thirteen from the Sermon on the Mount. Especially worthy of note are the famous words from the preface to his collected sermons:

I want to know one thing, the way to heaven: how to land safe on that happy shore. God himself has condescended to teach the way; for this very end he came from heaven. He hath written it down in a book! I have it; here is knowledge enough for me. Let me be *homo unius libri*. Here then I am, far from the busy ways of men. I sit down alone; only God is here. In his presence I open, I read this book; for this end, to find the way to heaven. Is there a doubt concerning the meaning of what I read? Does anything appear dark or intricate? I lift up my heart to the Father of lights. Lord, is it not thy word, "If any man lack wisdom, let him ask of God"? . . . . Thou hast said, "If any be willing to do thy will, he shall know." I am willing to do thy will; let me know thy will.

---

[15] Seven volumes, New York, 1853; see I, xix.

NON-LITURGICAL LEADERS

The Reformed Church, in her various branches, goes back to John Calvin (1509-64). If he could have read such a statement he would have protested that back of him was the Bible, or rather, the Living Christ. At the fountainhead of the Reformed Church, in the city of Geneva, Calvin set up lofty ideals of scholarly preaching. As a popular speaker he was scarcely in the same class with Luther, but as a scholarly interpreter the iron man of Geneva was second to none. His commentaries came out of his daily preaching. While he spoke extemporaneously, still "he spoke literature." Hence Beza once said of Calvin's sermons, "Every word weighs a pound." [16] Even to this hour his commentaries throw a flood of light upon the open Book, but as practical object lessons of how to preach, his written words sometimes lack warmth.

There was no lack of warmth, or even heat, in the pulpit work of Calvin's follower and friend, John Knox (1505-72), who was virtually the founder of the Presbyterian Church. Knox is said to have combined something of "the statesmanship of Calvin with the fiery eloquence of Savonarola." Like Calvin, Knox was a diligent student of the Bible, and of the best books available. For example, he used Chrysostom on Saint Matthew. Like Chrysostom, Knox was a fearless reformer. In the pulpit he might have taken as his motto the words of Jeremiah: "Is not my word like as a fire, saith the Lord; and like a hammer that breaketh the rocks in pieces?" [17]

By such preaching John Knox shook the land of Scotland,

---

[16] *"Tot verba tot pondera."*
[17] Jer. 23:29.

which prior to his day was Roman Catholic. Largely by his preaching he brought about the Scottish Reformation. But the three sermons which are extant scarcely accord with his reputation. Like many another popular preacher, he must have spoken to be heard. Surely he did not write to be read. But partly because of his influence, the Presbyterian Churches have always stressed preaching, and nowhere more than in Scotland. At Free St. George's, Edinburgh, for instance, there has been a long succession of able preachers, notably Alexander Whyte (1836-1931), a brilliant expositor.[18]

Ablest of all Presbyterian preachers was probably Thomas Chalmers (1780-1847). This brilliant young Scotch minister first settled at Kilmany, a rural parish. There for seven years his ministry lacked power. But after a sort of homiletical regeneration he began to preach Christ. In the earlier days of his ministry a frank lay friend told him, "I find you aye busy, but come when I may, I never find you at your studies for the Sabbath." This was the reply, "Oh, an hour or two on the Saturday evening is quite enough for that." But after the change of heart in Chalmers, this same friend often found him poring over the open pages of the Bible. "I never come in now, sir, but I find you aye at your Bible." "All too little, John, all too little!"

Meanwhile, the parish of Kilmany was being transformed. For seven years Chalmers had been mildly expostulating with his people about their shortcomings, but all to no avail. When he began to preach Christ as he makes himself known in the Book, the parish thief turned from his pilfering, the drunkard gave up his cups, and the worldling began to be a saint.

---

[18] See *Life of Alexander Whyte*, by G. F. Barbour, Doran, 1924.

In the famous sermon which Chalmers preached when he was bidding farewell to Kilmany, to enter upon a distinguished career at Glasgow, St. Andrews, and Edinburgh, he said near the close: "You have at least taught me that to preach Christ is the only effective way to preach morality in all its branches." [19]

In a somewhat different way the leading ministers of the Baptist Churches have been worthy of note for their use of the Bible in preaching. Chief among the mighty Baptist preachers to the common people was John Bunyan (1628-88). In more recent times Charles Haddon Spurgeon (1834-92) became probably the most influential pastoral preacher since the days of the Apostles. According to the late Sir William Robertson Nicoll, editor of *The British Weekly,* and a learned bookman, every young minister in the English-speaking world ought to saturate his soul in the sermons of Spurgeon, and thus learn the secrets of a soul-winning and life-building ministry.

More rewarding would be a course of home study in the written work of Alexander McLaren (1826-1910), of Manchester, England. By common consent this Baptist divine was "the prince of expositors." [20] With deep piety, sound learning, and scholarly habits of study, he combined a winsome personality and noteworthy gifts as a speaker. He prepared for each sermon even more carefully than if he had planned to read his message, or else speak from memory. While the words welled up from his heart at the moment of utterance, they flowed out of a heart filled with waters drawn from

---

[19] *Memoirs of Thomas Chalmers,* by William Hanna, Edinburgh, 1854, I, 197, 327.
[20] See *Dr. McLaren of Manchester,* by Miss E. T. McLaren, Hodder & Stoughton, London, 1911.

the wells of salvation, and out of a life filled with the Spirit of Christ.

Another denomination which has been notable for the high quality of her preaching is the Congregational Church. Among the most brilliant of her pulpit expositors was Joseph Parker (1830-1902), of City Temple, London. Safer as examples for the parish minister would be William M. Taylor (1828-95) and Charles E. Jefferson (1860-1937). Each of them attained distinction as the pastor of the Broadway Tabernacle, New York City. In the Yale Lectures by William M. Taylor [21] there is a helpful chapter on "Expository Preaching." At the Broadway Tabernacle it was his custom on every Lord's Day to preach one sermon that was expository and one that was topical.

As for Charles E. Jefferson, his writings about homiletics and kindred subjects [22] have inspired a whole generation of pastoral preachers. At the Broadway Tabernacle week after week for thirty-two years he kept feeding his flock. As a consequence his Sunday morning congregation seemed to the visitor like one large family gathered from the ends of Greater New York. While he was showing a host of younger men how to preach, he looked upon himself primarily as "the ministering shepherd." Like every other true pastor, his chief concern here below was for the sheep, one by one.

Thus we have looked at some of the founders and former leaders in various branches of the Church. These are only

---

[21] *The Ministry of the Word*, New York, 1883, pp. 153-180. His expository writings include *The Parables* and *The Miracles;* his topical sermons, *Contrary Winds* and *The Limitations of Life.*

[22] E.g., *The Building of the Church*, Macmillan, 1913, and *The Minister as Prophet*, Crowell, 1905.

a few of the many who have preached from the Bible so as to meet the needs of men. The ministry of such men has repeatedly shown the fulfillment of the ancient promise:

As the rain cometh down and the snow from heaven, and returneth not thither, but watereth the earth, and causeth it to bring forth and bud, that it may give seed to the sower and bread to the eater, so shall my word be that goeth forth from my mouth; it shall not return unto me void, but it shall accomplish that which I please, and prosper in the thing whereto I sent it.[23]

Since this promise still holds good, there is in the Book abundance of seed-corn for the pastor's study and of nourishing food for the people's souls.

BIBLICAL PREACHERS TODAY

What is the status of biblical preaching in our country today? According to some observers, especially from across the sea, there is among us a famine, "not a famine of bread, nor a thirst for water, but of hearing the words of the Lord."[24] A careful survey of the field, however, would show that in every branch of the Church more than a few ministers are basing their preaching upon the Bible, and that the number of such men seems to be growing from year to year. At present we can merely glance at a few representative preachers.

Let us begin with the Congregationalists, who have recently merged with the Christian Church. The Secretary of the new denomination is Douglas Horton, of Chicago. In his book *Taking a City*,[25] written while he was still a pastor,

---

[23] Isa. 55:10, 11.
[24] Amos 8:11; cf. I Sam. 3:1 (A.R.V. margin).
[25] Harper, 1934, pp. 1-13.

the opening sermon is about the spiritual needs of Chicago. As Lord Bryce once warned us,[26] if our civilization ever goes on the rocks, the catastrophe will come because we have failed to manage and govern our cities. In view of such facts and fears, what shall the city pastor say? Instead of contenting himself with silence about the sins of his city, or with heated denunciations of civic conditions in general, let him study this message about taking a modern city for God.

After a brief, gripping introduction, which sets forth the spiritual plight of the city, the minister asks his people, in substance, "How can we in the Church impart a soul to Chicago?" The answer is fourfold. It embodies the sort of meaningful repetition which often marks the sermons of Harry Emerson Fosdick. In substance the answer about Chicago is as follows: If we are to save our city we must have the Bible—the Bible with the Gospel—the Bible with the Gospel which culminates in the Resurrection of Christ— the Bible which culminates in the Resurrection of Christ, and with a host of witnesses to make this Gospel known to everyone in our city.

More directly biblical is a recent book by Frederick K. Stamm, of Brooklyn, a prominent minister of the Reformed Church. The title is *The Conversations of Jesus*.[27] This book seems to have grown out of Sunday morning sermons over the radio from coast to coast, under the heading "Highlights of the Bible." In the book, although the author carefully limits the field, there are sermons about fifty-seven different conversations of our Lord. This sort of preaching from the

---

[26] *The American Commonwealth*, Macmillan, 1911, I, 628-39.
[27] Harper, 1939.

Gospels may well fill up any minister's Sunday morning program during a good deal of the year, notably in the harvest season, which comes between New Year's and Easter.

Among the Methodists, too, there is a growing concern about preaching from the Bible. During the recent Preaching Mission, whose leaders were from various branches of the church, no one was more active than E. Stanley Jones, whose preaching is filled with the spiritual essence of the Book. In the now happily reunited Methodist Church there is a feeling that the brethren from the South will bring with them a welcome spirit of devotion to the Bible, with old-fashioned Wesleyan passion for the winning of souls. One of these brethren in the South is Clovis G. Chappell, who is now at St. Luke's Church, Oklahoma City. In 1922 he sent forth the first of his books with a title which points directly to the Scriptures.[28] Almost every year he has been sending out a volume of such sermons.[29]

Among Presbyterians the same line of thought applies to Clarence E. Macartney, of the First Church, Pittsburgh. In 1916 he sent out the first of his books with a title pointing directly to the Book.[30] From that time to this, especially since the collapse of the business boom in 1929, he has brought forth a new book of sermons almost every year.[31] In the Presbyterian Church, U. S., commonly known as the Southern Church, one of many biblical preachers is Harris E. Kirk, of Franklin Street Church, Baltimore. Unlike Macartney, whose pulpit work attracts throngs of people of every sort—

---

[28] *Sermons on Biblical Characters,* Doran, 1922.
[29] E.g., *Sermons from the Miracles,* Cokesbury, 1937.
[30] *Parables of the Old Testament,* Revell, 1916.
[31] E.g., *Peter and His Lord,* Cokesbury, 1937.

notably young people and mature men—the Baltimore minister appeals rather to the exceptional man, such as the judge, or the professor at Johns Hopkins Medical School.

For example, take a little volume of ten sermons [32] in which Kirk uses facts about Jacob in order to preach truths about God. Among all the books in this current series, which is monthly, no volume seems more worthy of note as an object lesson of preaching from the Bible. The interesting fact is that both Kirk and Macartney, differing as they do both in temperament and in theology, have been preaching from the Bible for years. With them for convenience one may mention Oscar F. Blackwelder, at the downtown Lutheran Church of the Reformation, Washington, D. C.

In the Protestant Episcopal Church, also, there is a movement toward the increased use of the Bible in preaching. At the General Seminary in New York City two professors have written a book [33] showing Episcopalian clergymen how to preach from the passages set apart as readings throughout the Church Year. In the same city until recently the rector of Grace Church was W. Russell Bowie, who is now professor of preaching at Union Theological Seminary. When he was installed he spoke on the subject "The Authority Back of Our Preaching." That authority is from the Bible. The Bible alone, says the professor, voices "the everlasting messages of the world's hope."

Finally, let us think about George W. Truett, of the First Baptist Church, Dallas, Texas. Whether he is ad-

---

[32] *A Man of Property, or the Jacob Saga*, Harper, 1935.
[33] *The Eternal Word in the Modern World*, by B. S. Easton and H. C. Robbins, Scribner, 1937.

dressing a throng of unconverted cattlemen out on the Texas range, or a still larger gathering of his friends at the home church, his constant dependence is upon the grace of God, as revealed in Christ. His preaching is notable for simplicity and persuasiveness.[34]

Thus we have glanced at representative preachers of yesterday and today. As one star differeth from every other star in glory, so has every one of our chosen preachers differed from all the rest, both in personality and in preaching style. But they have all been alike in devotion to the Bible and in preaching from it as the God-given means of helping the man in the pew. Evidently there is no one standarized way of preaching from the Book. "Where the Spirit of the Lord is, there is liberty." [35] In such freedom there is power, the power of God flowing through the man of his choice. The Spirit-filled preacher, then, is the one who speaks with power, because he speaks for God.

---

[34] See his sermons, *Follow Thou Me,* Harper, 1935, and the biography, *George W. Truett,* by Powhatan W. James, Macmillan, 1939.
[35] II Cor. 3:17*b*.

CHAPTER II

THE PRESENT-DAY VARIETIES

LET us pause now and get our bearings. In view of the examples at which we have looked, what is biblical preaching? Sometimes we talk about such sermons as though they were all alike. In a sense they are. Whatever the form, biblical preaching is ever the same in spirit. But since we are concerned with the art of preaching, as well as the subject matter, we should give some attention to the varieties of biblical sermons. While these forms are as diverse as the stars at midnight, each star keeps on being a star, and nothing but a star. In like manner, every biblical sermon should be a sermon, and nothing but a sermon. What, then, is a biblical sermon? How can we distinguish among the various kinds? Evidently we must employ a few terms which are technical.

"But why should we have to bother with homiletical distinctions? Are they not artificial, even arbitrary?" Alas, ofttimes they are! But every art has its technical terms, which are clear to the master of the art; and preaching is no exception. Certain terms have long been in use among the masters of the preacher's craft. Let us therefore look at a few of these terms, especially those which have to do with biblical preaching. Then let us inquire about the sources of the variety which makes these terms necessary. Ere long we should begin to thank God for a variety as pleasing as that of the flower beds in an old-fashioned garden.

34

What, then, is "preaching." According to Phillips Brooks, preaching is "the bringing of truth through personality." Brooks found the truth primarily in the Scriptures. But he would not have agreed with certain zealous ministers who aver that one should preach "nothing but the Bible," in the sense that one should ignore all other books and sources of truth. If in every sermon the biblical truth should be present, much as the wheat is in the loaf, in order to impart the life-giving power, various other elements should enter in, if only to supply the human flavor. Hence there is in good preaching untold variety, and there ought to be even more.

Again, what is "a sermon"? According to a famous definition, a sermon is "an oral address to the popular mind, upon religious truth contained in the Scriptures, and elaborately treated with a view to persuasion."[1] Except for the one word, "elaborately," the definition is admirable. For this word let us substitute "attractively," or even "simply." In preaching, the truth should be attractively treated with a view to persuasion! As F. W. Robertson says, "Preach suggestively, not exhaustively." Robertson believed in preaching from the Bible. But he stressed the preaching, not the exposition. He did not deem it wise to overload the sermon, even though the excess weight might come from the Scriptures. In other words, whenever a man preaches, he should preach!

A familiar term which sometimes causes confusion is "the topical sermon." In one sense of the term, it is wholly good. Almost every popular sermon, however biblical the content,

---

[1] Austin Phelps, *The Theory of Preaching*, Scribner, 1881, pp. 1-27. This is probably the best of the older textbooks on homiletics.

should have its topic—the more attractive the better, provided it is true. For example, look at two volumes of sermons by well-known preachers in Glasgow: *The Cross in Christian Experience,* by William M. Clow,[2] and *The Hero in Thy Soul,* by Arthur J. Gossip.[3] Each book owes its popular favor in no small degree to the attractive title. In each book almost every sermon has an arresting topic. This one is from the book by Clow, "The Cross and the Conscience"; and this one from the book by Gossip, "When Life Tumbles In, What Then?"

In the technical sense, a topical sermon is one which owes its form to the unfolding of the truth wrapped up in the title. That sounds harmless. So it is. Indeed, it is refreshing, when the truth wrapped up in the title is worthy, and when the unfolding is in keeping with our holy faith. In the history of the Christian pulpit, practically every sermon which has become famous has been topical.[4] Why, then, do advocates of biblical preaching sometimes find fault with the topical sermon? In so far as they are wise, as often they are not, such critics object to the topical sermon only when it is secular, either in substance or in spirit. In other words, they feel that the vital thing in a sermon is the spiritual message, not the striking topic.

Another term which causes confusion is "the textual sermon." In the popular sense of the term, almost every sermon from the average pulpit is textual. Partly out of respect for tradition, and likewise because of deference to the Bible, the

---

[2] Doran, 1911.
[3] Scribner, 1930.
[4] E.g., Horace Bushnell's famous sermon, "Every Man's Life a Plan of God," in *Sermons for the New Life,* London, 1892, pp. 1-15.

minister usually starts to preach by announcing his text. In the course of the sermon he may refer to it at times, and even repeat it word for word. Still the message may or may not be "textual." When the sermon is textual, in fact as in name, the minister is interpreting the truth enshrined in his text. In order to interpret, he must do more than merely echo or quote. Whenever he properly interprets and illuminates a text in a helpful message for today, he finds that this sort of preaching is as fruitful now as in days of old. If in this book there is little about the textual sermon, under that heading, the reason is that the facts are well known to every student of homiletics.

The textual sermon, in the technical sense, is one in which the structure follows the order of the ideas in the text. This is the sort of preaching in which F. W. Robertson excelled. Every one of his textual sermons—which serve in the seminary as models of how to preach—has its accurate topic. For example, think of these subjects: "The Loneliness of Christ," "The Irreparable Past," and "The Principle of the Spiritual Harvest." Each of these sermons is notable for sturdy structure. As a rule the structure follows the order of the ideas in the text, though sometimes Robertson transposes the two parts. So much does he emphasize the text that if the hearer remembers it he will recall the structure of the sermon. If he remembers the drift of the sermon he will recall the text. Whenever such a man preaches, one of his aims is to leave in the hearer's Bible and in his heart another illuminated text.

Still another term, which appears in the books less frequently than it should, is "the biographical sermon." In fact, the books on preaching say practically nothing about this fascinating way of presenting divine truth and human duty. The idea is to select a biblical character—preferably one who is well known, such as Gideon in Judges—and then use some of the facts about him as the basis for a moving sermon. Such a sermon stresses one large truth, or one impelling duty. For instance, if the pastor of a congregation with three hundred members wishes to preach about aggressive teamwork for God, where can he find a better passage than the one about Gideon's band of three hundred? [5]

EXPOSITORY PREACHING TERMS

A much more elusive term is "the expository sermon." In the broad sense, this sort of sermon is the unfolding of the truth contained in a passage longer than two or three consecutive verses. Often the unit is a single paragraph. Again the chosen passage may be a chapter, or some other cluster of paragraphs. Occasionally the sermon has to do with an entire book of the Bible. As a rule the structure of the expository sermon follows the order of the ideas in the passage, but not slavishly. The emphasis is on the preaching, not the exposition. Hence one does not go into the pulpit to "preach the Bible." While one should preach "from the Bible," the heart of the message should be about God in Christ. If one has a sufficient reason for transposing the order of the materials, or else omitting some of them altogether, there is nothing in homiletics to hamper one's freedom. Homiletics is the orderly statement of the principles which master preachers have followed in presenting the Gospel, and with few exceptions the master interpreters of the Book have been

---

[5] Judg. 7:2 et p.

expository preachers only in this broader sense of the term. According to the present book, therefore, any pulpit message which is based on a fairly long biblical passage is an expository sermon.

Meanwhile there is a widespread impression that the expository sermon is simply a verse-by-verse explanation of a chosen passage. For example, in a well-known collection of sermons by master preachers, the one by Martin Luther is "The Methods and Fruits of Justification." [6] The first part of the discourse has to do with the doctrine in general; the latter part deals with each of the seven verses separately. Both the passage and the doctrine are difficult. But in the hands of such a master as Luther the resulting sermon is worthy of note. This sort of preaching still proves helpful, provided the man in the pulpit has both gifts and charm, and the people have both the ability to think and the desire to learn. Nevertheless, it would be a pity if verse-by-verse explanation were the only type of expository preaching.

Again, there is a popular impression that the expository preacher must work his way straight through the book in hand. For instance, take William M. Taylor's definition: "By expository preaching I mean that method of pulpit discourse which consists in the consecutive interpretation and practical enforcement of a book in the sacred canon." [7] Surely there is a place for this kind of preaching, as we shall see ere long. But no less surely there should be a place for the occasional sermon, or series of sermons, when one has not sufficient time or opportunity to deal with an entire book,

---

[6] Gal. 4:1-7. *The World's Great Sermons,* compiled by Grenville Kleiser, 10 vols., Funk, New York, 1908, I, 113-143.
[7] *The Ministry of the Word,* New York, 1883, p. 155.

section by section. For example, think of a minister on a circuit, in which he visits a certain station only once a month. How long would it take him to deal adequately with the Gospel of Luke? On the other hand, why should he not be able to preach a helpful expository sermon about the parable of the lost sheep? [8]

Sometimes it is the ability which is limited. Who among us would dare to embark on a popular verse-by-verse exposition of the Apocalypse, or to deal with the whole book by chapters? On the other hand, there should be no difficulty in dealing with certain passages. Better still, one could prepare a series of popular sermons from the letters to the seven churches, under the heading, "What Jesus Says to the City Church." [9] From the point of view in the present book, this is usually the most satisfactory way to prepare and preach expository sermons. Meanwhile the emphasis is upon the freedom of the pulpit expositor to deal with the Bible as seems to him best in view of his own ability and his people's highest welfare. Let him never submit to bondage under any theory of preaching.

Nevertheless, there is a place and a need for "the expository lecture." In fact, this is the expository sermon par excellence. During the old days in Scotland it was the custom for the dominie to preach a textual sermon in the morning, and to give an expository lecture in the afternoon. Of the two discourses the expository lecture was usually the more welcome to the mature hearer, because it brought him closer to the

---

[8] Luke 15:1-7.

[9] Rev. 2, 3. See *Letters to the Seven Churches,* by Sir Wm. Ramsay, Doran, 1905; and *Commentary on the Epistles to the Seven Churches,* by Richard C. Trench, London, 1883.

heart of the Book. That was where he found God. To this day, wherever the minister has the ability and the training, and wherever parish conditions permit, no other sermons throughout the year will prove more rewarding to both pastor and people than the course of popular expository lectures.

By a "course" one means a number of sermons given from week to week at the same service, whether morning or evening, but not announced as a series. By this other term "series" one refers to a number of consecutive sermons given at the same hour on successive Sundays, usually at night, and previously announced as a unified whole. The difference between the two terms is that in a course the emphasis is upon the individual sermon, whereas in a series the stress is upon the whole. In a course the element of continuity may be secondary, but in a series there ought to be both continuity and climax. Unlike the course, which calls little attention to itself, the series ought to be an event in the spiritual history of the parish.

As a rule the pastor relies much more upon courses than upon series. As a teaching minister he is likely to have some sort of course running practically all the time. On the other hand, he may announce a special series only once in a while, perhaps once a quarter. The underlying theory is that special events are more likely to prove effective if they do not come close together. Each one should shine in its own light. Unless a man is unusually gifted as a serial preacher he will find that in a congregation with a stable constituency one series after another tends to prove monotonous.

In a downtown church, however, there need be no such concern. If the minister knows how to plan different sorts of series, and how to preach every sermon in it as a unified message straight from the throne, he can have one series in the morning and another at night. He can keep on having series after series, both morning and evening, as long as he has something to say that is worthy of special note. By dignified publicity and in other ways not spectacular he can appeal to a cross section of perhaps a million people. Under God, his effectiveness as a preacher depends a good deal upon his ability to attract strangers and make them feel at home in his church. For such a difficult ministry the popular series of biblical sermons is a gift from heaven.

Thus we have looked at various technical terms. Of course there are others. But surely we have looked at enough! If some of them should come out in the wash on blue Monday, no lasting harm would result. Almost every term mentioned above is open to different interpretations, and some of the terms overlap. For example, in a worthy volume by Alexander McLaren, *The Secret of Power*,[10] the sermon which gives the title to the book is topical in announcement, expository in substance, and textual in treatment. Such biblical homiletics is typical of McLaren. No matter how long his passage, he always has a popular title, and a memorable text, which is usually brief. No matter how brief the text, he almost invariably preaches the substance of the surrounding paragraph, or of several consecutive paragraphs. As Henry Ward Beecher used to say, such a preacher uses his text as a gateway into a fertile field, but he wastes no time swinging on the gate.

The one term which includes all these varieties, and every-

---

[10] Macmillan, London, 1882, pp. 1-25.

thing else of the sort, is "the biblical sermon." The biblical sermon is the popular interpretation of divine truth and human duty as revealed in the Scriptures. Except in the occasional "Bible reading," where one feels free to flit from passage to passage, the biblical message almost always comes primarily from a single unit of Scripture. Otherwise one might form the habit of "going everywhere preaching the Gospel." By using the hop-skip-and-jump method of sermonizing, one might form the habit of using the concordance to chase a chosen word through the Scriptures, without ever pausing to explain any one passage. But whenever one is actually interpreting the scripture in hand, the aim is to let the truth of God shine out through the sermon so as to illumine the soul of the layman and thus lead him in doing the will of the Heavenly Father. This is the sort of preaching for which many laymen are asking.

Among the biblical messages in any one pulpit from week to week, there should be wholesome variety. For example, Arthur J. Gossip has a sermon under the title, "What Christ Means by a Good Man." [11] The chosen passage consists of thirty-two verses from the Sermon on the Mount. Throughout the sermon, in each of the twenty paragraphs, the warp of the message is from this one part of the Scriptures. The woof is from the life and thought of our day, with continuous reference to the interests and needs of the man in the pew. On the other hand, the volume contains an even more suggestive and helpful sermon drawn from a single text. The subject is, "The Art of Thinking in Terms of the Cross." From the present point of view, this message is as biblical

---

[11] *The Hero in Thy Soul*, Scribner, 1930, pp. 77-90, 130-43.

as the other. In short, there are countless ways of preaching helpfully from the Bible.

What, then, are the sources of wholesome variety among biblical sermons? Without pausing to list them all, we may single out four. Two of them have to do with the Bible, and two concern the preacher. Let us begin with the Bible.

VARIED BIBLICAL SOURCES

The first source of wholesome variety is in the character of the biblical materials. For example, a sermon from Genesis should differ from a message about the Lord Jesus as he makes himself known in the Gospel of John. Even more should a message from Ruth be unlike a sermon from the Epistle to the Hebrews. A message from the first chapter of Isaiah, about God's judgment on the nation, should not closely resemble a sermon from the fortieth chapter, about God's mercy to his people. The same is true of Paul's letter to the Romans. There is almost as much difference between the "tone color" of the two main parts as there is between the early and the latter part of Shakespeare's *Winter's Tale*. Hence the wise interpreter hesitates to preach from any section of a Bible book until he knows something about the book as a whole. On the other hand, when he becomes familiar with any book in the Bible as one of his closest friends, this knowledge of the book as a whole should help him in making the resulting message both popular and dynamic.

The second source of variety is in the character of the chosen passage. For example, there is a most suggestive book dealing with the preaching values in Genesis 12–50.[12]

---

[12] *Hebrew Ideals*, by James Strahan, Edinburgh, 1915.

44

While they are not closely expository, the various discussions are often illuminating. These are the headings of the first fifteen parts: Ideals, Separations, Blessedness, Worship, Truth, Decision, Warfare, Peace, Assurance, Grace, Patience, Compassion, Power, Hospitality, Education. These ten, arranged in pairs, come from other parts of the book: Mercy, Judgment; Laughter, Tears; Love, Home; Honor, Conscience; Farewell, Faith. The book as a whole contains forty-six sections. They in turn suggest subjects enough to keep a man busy on Sunday morning for more than a year, without undue repetition.

In any sermon the method of treatment depends partly on the length of the passage. When one preaches from a text which is short, with little reference to what comes before and after, one has time to take up the parts in detail. For example, in dealing with "The Golden Text of the Bible" [18] one can single out such a meaningful word as "so" or "whosoever" and hold it up to view. When one is preaching from a paragraph—it may be a parable, such as that about the Good Samaritan—one should paint with a larger brush. When one deals with a chapter, such as Hebrews eleven, one needs to know what to omit, or else pass over quickly, in order to bring out the central lesson. Some day, when one dares to give a bird's-eye view of an entire book, such as Mark, one needs to have rare synthesizing powers, and still rarer gifts of omission. Effectiveness in popular interpretation of the Bible depends largely on having one high purpose for each discourse, and on willingness to omit everything else. In short, the biblical preacher should be wiser than Solomon.

---

[18] John 3:16.

In view of such varied materials, why is a man's preaching from the Bible likely to be notable for sameness, tameness, and lameness? Such pulpit work is a misrepresentation of God's Holy Book. The Bible itself is like a land of hills and valleys. During any one year, or any one quarter, the minister should lead his friends into various parts of this enchanting country. If he tarries with the same congregation for ten years, which is probably long enough, his pulpit work should keep on being different every time he preaches. If he is such an exceptional man as to linger in the same parish forty years and still not wear out his welcome, he should find in the Scriptures more materials than he needs to keep from undue repetition of the same sermons, or even the same kinds of sermons. In short, the more one preaches from the Bible, the more one finds to preach.

DIFFERENT PREACHING PERSONALITIES

Another source of wholesome variety among sermons from the Book is in the personality of the preacher. Under God, the preacher is an artist. When he looks into some portion of the Bible, he ought to preach what he finds. What he finds depends almost as much upon his personality as upon the character of the passage. For example, over on the hillside in August four men are painting the same landscape. As each of them makes his preliminary sketch, and then quickly limns in his colors, he keeps talking with his three friends. At the end of the day, each of them carries home a painting which differs widely from the other three pictures. So it must always be with creative endeavor. If any man's work is not his own, he is merely a copyist, not an artist.

The variety among biblical sermons, therefore, is due largely to differences of preaching viewpoints. For example, on the desk are four sermons by different preachers. Each of them is interpreting the most wondrous of the parables.[14] Each man goes somewhat into the facts of the parable; but still no two of the messages are alike, either in substance or in spirit. The sermon about "The Joy with God" is by Phillips Brooks. Here, as elsewhere, he is an irrepressible optimist, one of "those happy preachers." The message about "The Hunger of the Soul" is by Horace Bushnell, perhaps the ablest of American preachers. With his amazing insight into the meaning of human experience, especially in its somber hues, he might be called "a biblical realist." Opinions may differ about which of these two sermons is closer to the heart of the parable. Neither of them is like a third message, "The Prodigal's Return," by Charles H. Spurgeon. In this sermon, as elsewhere, Spurgeon combines the "biblical realism" of Bushnell with the "apostolic optimism" of Brooks. Fortunately the optimism prevails; Spurgeon too was one of "those happy preachers." Not many miles distant from his Tabernacle was Robert William Dale, at Carr's Lane, Birmingham. In his distinctive fashion Dale was a power. When he brought out a sermon from this parable his subject was "The Doctrine of the Atonement." Under God, one reason why each of those four contemporaries became a master preacher was that he dared to be himself.

Still another source of variation lies in the minister's purpose. If he so desired, he could preach from this parable a score of times, and use every sermon in meeting a different need of

---

[14] Luke 15:11-32.

the human heart. In a certain parish the officers used to say to the parson playfully, "Whenever you run out of anything else to preach, you fall back on the fifteenth chapter of Luke. But we never get tired of hearing about the Prodigal Son, for we are like him ourselves." So is every man, more or less, apart from the grace of God. Hence the layman is glad to learn that this parable is about "The Love of Our Father God." In fact, this may be the topic of the sermon.

In the parable the leading character is the father. As in Judah's moving plea for the life of his brother, Benjamin,[15] the word father rings out in the parable repeatedly, ten times in all. While there is not an allusion to the Cross, the heart of the Gospel is here. In a sense, the whole chapter rests beneath the shadow of the Cross, for in Luke these three parables about the finding of the sinner come shortly before the account of the Saviour's death. Indeed, the heavenly Father sent his Son into our own far country, where each of us is a sinner. That Son died to bring each of us back to his senses, and thus back to the heart of God.[16]

As a rule, however, it is best to preach the parable as it stands, each time from a different point of view. These five topics are about the Loving Father: "The Father of the Prodigal," "The Father God and His Sons," "The Forgiveness of Sins," "The Gifts that Accompany Forgiveness," and "The Joys of Finding the Lost." Such preaching should help to restore the balance in our thinking about God. Many of us seem to agree with little Mary, who said, "Mamma, I like Jesus better than I like God." "Why, Mary, that is awful!"

---

[15] Gen. 44:18-34.
[16] Cf. the novel *My Son, My Son,* by Howard Spring, Viking, New York, 1938, suggested by II Sam. 18:33.

"No, Mamma, Jesus has done more for us!" Then Mary's mother should have told her that in the New Testament almost every golden text about salvation begins with God the Father.[17] As a rule the emphasis is upon his love for us sinners, one by one. Even when he is said to love the world, the stress is upon "whosoever." What a Gospel!

In the parable, second only to the loving father is the erring son. This word son rings forth again and again, nine times in all. These facts may lead to a sermon "The Temptations of the Prodigal Son," or else "Why the Young Man Leaves the Farm." In practically every rural parish this is a serious problem. Now as of old, the city lures in four different ways: "Young man, you have too much work, too little play, too few jolly companions of your own age, and too little chance to spend money. Come to the city and have a good time." Alas, that usually means a bad time. In the city, at least during a boom, there may seem to be little need for work, no lack of play, no end of jolly good fellows, as well as bad women, and no limit to the amount of money to be squandered in sin. But all the while the books of life are being kept with meticulous care. Sooner or later the reckoning will come. Even from the point of view of the world, sin does not pay; or rather, it pays with coins minted in hell.

Again there may be a sermon about "The Psychology of Conversion." "When he came to himself!" "What a phrase! Among all the writers of the New Testament, Luke is the practical psychologist. His fifteenth chapter likewise suggests a sermon about "The Meaning of Repentance." According

---

[17] E.g., John 3:16; Rom. 5:8; II Cor. 5:19.

to Gipsy Smith, Sr., the difference between repentance and conversion is like the difference between awaking in the morning and getting up. "I will arise!" This is a sort of New Year's resolution, which ought to mark the beginning of a new life. Then there may be a message about "The Confession of Sins." "Father, I have sinned!"

Even more heart-searching may be the sermon about "The Temptations of the Mature Man." The average man in "The Middle Passage of the Years"[18] is more like the elder brother than like the prodigal. The temptations of the typical self-respecting man past forty-five years of age have to do with work and play, love and money. He may be proud because he works hard and plays not at all, because he wastes no time with boon companions and squanders no money. If so, he is a sinner, perhaps worse than his wastrel brother. The sins of the spirit are even deadlier than those of the flesh. The sins of such a middle-aged man are those of the Pharisee: pride in himself, unwillingness to forgive his penitent brother, and ingratitude toward their loving father—that is, toward God. In reading the parable aloud, listen for the supercilious "I," the contemptuous "he," and the ungracious "thou." Is not a man's use of personal pronouns a fairly reliable index of his character? In fact, is not the Third Gospel a portrait gallery filled with revelations of human weakness and divine grace?

Thus we have looked at four sources of variety among biblical messages. Since there are numberless ways of securing wholesome variety, there should be in the pulpit no room for

---

[18] For a sermon about the perils of middle age see J. D. Jones, *The Gospel of the Sovereignty*, Hodder & Stoughton, 1914, pp. 301-313. For a popular psychological treatment see A. Herbert Gray, *About People*, Scribner, 1934.

a succession of sermons as much alike as an assembly line of low-priced cars. Mechanical sermons, if indeed they be sermons, are usually the handiwork of a homiletical carpenter. Probably he is a copyist. Even if he imitated the written work of F. W. Robertson and Alexander McLaren, the resulting "sermons" would be wooden. As a rule, however, the mechanical sermonizer does not take time to study the methods of any master preacher, but rather builds wooden work according to rules laid down in a book. From this point of view there are only two ways of preaching from the Bible. The one way is good, because the message is vital. The other is bad, because the finished product is made by machine.

Whatever the form, real preaching is vital. It lives. It moves. It leads the hearer to do the will of God. It makes him feel as the two disciples felt on the road to Emmaus. On the way home from church next Sunday morning, after the minister has delivered one of his soul-stirring messages, the thoughtful deacon should say to his wife, "Did not our heart burn within us, while he talked with us by the way, and while he opened to us the Scriptures?" [19]

What, then, does it mean for the man in the pulpit to open the Book? It means to let the light of the knowledge of the glory of God in the face of Jesus Christ shine out through the preacher and his sermon. Like the Apostle Paul, such a preacher is only an earthen vessel. But when the vessel is cleansed by the Spirit of God, and is flooded with light from above, the man in the pew should behold the Living Christ as Saviour and Lord, and thus be transformed into his likeness.[20] This is the secret of Christian radiance.

---

[19] Luke 24:32.
[20] II Cor. 4:7; 3:18.

CHAPTER III

THE BIOGRAPHICAL SERMON

THE easiest way for the young minister to start preaching from the Bible may be to prepare a biographical sermon. If it is worthy, it is almost certain to be popular. It enables him to meet a host of human needs, one at a time. Best of all from the point of view of the beginner, such a message is comparatively easy to prepare. Of course the biographical sermon does not spring up of itself overnight while one sleeps. It is not like a succulent mushroom. But still this sort of pulpit fare is easier to make ready than most other kinds of biblical food. The wise young minister takes advantage of these facts and prepares a biographical sermon occasionally, perhaps once a month. For instance, if he is starting out on a circuit in the autumn, he may preach a number of Old Testament biographical sermons.

The biographical sermon is one which grows out of the facts concerning a biblical character, as these facts throw light upon the problems of the man in the pew. If this working description is broad, the reason is that there are different sorts of biographical sermons, even in the pulpit work of the same minister. For example, one has lived with Moses until one knows him well. In a time when our own land, like every other, is crying out for the strong man as leader, one looks upon Moses as the greatest man in the Old Testament. Sometimes he seems as big as a mountain. That is what one thinks after having gazed at Michelangelo's "Moses." The facts about him suggest many sermons.

The simplest sort of biographical sermon—the sort most likely to prove popular among a people whom one does not know—has to do with an episode in the life of a well-known hero. For instance, on Mother's Day one can preach about the way in which God watched over Baby Moses, and used his mother in sparing him for his life work. The text is, "Take this child away, and nurse it for me, and I will give thee thy wages." [1] What a dramatic scene! A strange woman, a princess, moved with pity by a baby's cry, offers the baby's mother wages for doing what her heart most longs to do. In the resulting sermon, without becoming sentimental or lachrymose, one can hold aloft the biblical ideal of motherhood. The subject is, "The Wages of a Godly Mother."

One of the most fruitful sermons on Moses should be about his discovery of God at the burning bush. [2] In almost every branch of the Presbyterian Church the burning bush is one of the official emblems. This fact suggests a sermon about the preservation of the Church in days of persecution, such as our friends have been enduring across the sea. "The bush burned with fire, and the bush was not consumed." The bush was God's way of making himself known to this ancient leader of men. God's way of making himself known now is often through the Church. As long as there are men who need to know the living God, the fires will keep burning on the altar of the Church.

A more popular line of thought has to do with "God's

---

[1] Exod. 2:9b. For a Mother's Day text see also Isa. 66:13a.
[2] Exod. 3:2b; or 3:5.

Cure for an Inferiority Complex." The materials are in two successive chapters,[3] where the man whom God is calling utters five excuses that sound strangely like the pretexts of a man today. In the sermon, however, the emphasis should be upon the way in which God answers each of these ingenious excuses, and at last sends the man of his choice out to engage in a hazardous life work. In such a sermon the human interest has to do with what one may call biblical psychology; but the divine power has to do with a man's religion, which centers in his God.

Someday one will dare to look at the life of this man in a broader and more difficult fashion. The subject may be, "How God Trains a Leader." [4] The facts about the life of Moses suggest three lines of thought, which one may present in the order of thesis, antithesis, synthesis. Thus the three parts of the sermon correspond with the three stages in the life of our hero. After an introduction in which one deals with the need of leadership in the nation now, one shows how God blesses such a man in the early years of prosperity, watches over him in the later years of obscurity (or adversity), and uses him in the long years of maturity. Strange to tell, this same line of thought applies also to the development of Joseph. In any such sermon, however, put the stress not on Moses, or Joseph, but on God.

In another broad sermon, with the same text, one may interpret the character of Moses as a strong man of God. Of course one should not use these two sermons close together, as the effect might be confusing. In this latter message the

---

[3] Exod. 3, 4.
[4] The text may be Deut. 34:10.

form may be textual. The first part of the text has to do with "the power of a human personality": "There arose not a prophet since in Israel like unto Moses." The basic idea here is that in the world before Christ the prophets were the mightiest of men. While Moses was more than a prophet, in a sense he was the first of that royal succession, and one of the greatest.[5] His power lay in his personality. Then as now, personality meant the ability to persuade people to do the will of God.

The latter part of the sermon is even more important. Here one deals with the words about Moses, "whom the Lord knew face to face." Thus the second heading may be, "the secret of a powerful personality." The secret is in God. Such a man is not born great and good; he becomes so by such old-fashioned means as faith and prayer and work. Here, then, is a typical Robertsonian sermon, which grows out of the two contrasting parts of a text as short as it is suggestive. F. W. Robertson often used such a text as a window through which he looked at the life of an Old Testament hero. But in the present-day sermon the emphasis would differ from that of Robertson, for he did not stress the concept of personality. So let us name the whole sermon "The Secret of a Powerful Personality."

POPULAR APPEAL

Whatever the form, if the biographical sermon is worthy of the name, it appeals to the average man of today. It appeals to his imagination and to his motor impulses. It lifts him out of himself and makes him determine to become the sort

---

[5] Deut. 18:15, 18.

of man God wishes him to be. In other words, the average layman is a hero worshiper. With wise old Samuel Johnson the layman often says, "The biographical part of literature is what I like best." During the week the layman may delve into books of secular biography. On Sunday he is delighted to discover that the new minister is familiar with the best books in this enchanting field. Such a minister is almost never at a loss for a telling illustration, because he knows the life of Sir Walter Scott or David Livingstone, as well as Alice Freeman Palmer or Helen Keller. Better still, the minister is able to make his biographical sermon as interesting and helpful as any secular biography. This is the sort of wide-awake man for whom more than one pulpit committee is searching.

The biographical sermon appeals to the layman for various reasons. One is that it comes out of the most interesting book in the world, and out of the most interesting part. In a popular work, written largely for the layman, our most refreshing lay preacher, William Lyon Phelps of Yale, writes about *Human Nature in the Bible*.[6] The discussion concerns human beings in the Old Testament, which records the experiences of men and women much like those in our pews. Instead of looking at them en masse, this lay writer deals with them as the Bible does, one at a time. Of course there are depths which the modern writer does not attempt to fathom, for in the Old Testament the basic message is about the glory of God's grace, not about the interest of human nature. But still the book does well what it starts out to do:

---

[6] Scribner, 1923.

it shows that the biographical parts of the Old Testament appeal to the modern man.

In Genesis, for example, there are pictures of human nature, both good and bad. Sometimes it seems to be chiefly bad. Since the evil is more fascinating than the good, one may preach occasionally about the men whom James M. Black calls *Rogues of the Bible*.[7] For example, take Esau. He was a sportsman. If he were living among us now he would shine as a forward in basketball, and as a halfback in football. Later in life he would continue to excel in hunting, in skiing, and in other manly sports. But he seems not to have been acceptable to God. Why? The resulting sermon should appeal to the young man whose native impulses are strong, as well as to the older man who remembers with shame the follies of his youth. The subject is, "The Man with No Religion."[8] Such a man is:

1. Concerned about things, not about persons.
2. Concerned about himself, not about others.
3. Concerned about his present, not about his future.
4. Concerned about himself, not about God.

Usually it is better to put the emphasis where the Bible puts it, upon the man who is doing the will of God. This is one reason why Genesis devotes more attention to Joseph than to all of its bad men put together. The minister who wishes to be popular, especially in preaching to young people, often turns to Joseph. He may not have been so profound

---

[7] Harper, 1930.

[8] Heb. 12:16. For a sermon about Esau see *The Forgiveness of Sins*, by George Adam Smith, Doran, 1905, pp. 174-91.

a personage as Moses, but Joseph too is interesting. His life story abounds in dramatic scenes. Whenever the man in the pulpit starts with a scene in the life of such a man, if the sermon measures up to its possibilities, the Spirit of God is waiting to use the message in moving the will of the hearer toward Christ.

The worthy biographical sermon is popular, again, because it is practical. In preaching about Esau, the practical purpose may be to set up danger signals at critical points along life's pathway, especially near the start. In preaching about the way in which Joseph met and conquered the most insidious temptation [9]—simply by appealing to God, and then by flight—the purpose may be to strengthen the young hearer for perils which he is sure to meet. Thus one can guide him in setting up the loftiest ideals, such as loyalty to God, to country, and to home, as well as to his friends, his work, and his ideals. For such a sermon the subject may be, "The Young Man's Religion."

The biographical sermon enables one to stress such old-fashioned habits as industry, friendliness, and optimism. These virtues all shone out from the life of Joseph. Between the years of seventeen and thirty he was a slave in a foreign land, a part of the time in prison. Except for the ideals which he had brought from the old home back on the farm, he might have become only a drudge. But he kept doing well whatever he found to do, winning friends among high and low, and living with hope in his heart. In the presence of these facts, why should one not be able to prepare a sermon which will shine?

---

[9] Gen. 39:9c.

In a practical sermon one preaches in the present tense. Instead of announcing that one will speak about the faithfulness of Joseph, one may choose as the topic "The Religion of the Businessman." Instead of preparing a long, dry, contextual introduction, one may start with the fact that in almost every city, and city church, the power is largely in the hands of the businessman. As an object lesson of what such a man should strive to become, one can deal with the facts about Joseph's career in business.

What, then, are the traits of the man who does the will of God in business today? He is notable for his character, especially for such business-like virtues as integrity, honesty, and truthfulness. He is noteworthy, also, for his service to his fellow-men. Like Joseph of old, the businessman is sometimes able to save the lives and the fortunes of his friends. All the while, he is a candidate for the life everlasting. By the grace of God he has a character and a sort of usefulness that are worthy of going on into the unseen world. In short, he is a good man. That is what the loved ones wish to say when the businessman has folded his hands for the last long sleep.

All of this, and vastly more, comes out of the truth as God makes it known through Joseph. His life and work are intensely practical, and yet he is a dreamer. Today he would be called a practical Christian idealist. This is largely what one means by "Religion as Loyalty."[10] Such a man's religion means that he is loyal to God amid the temptations of youth, the trials of early manhood, and the allurements of lofty station. Better still, such a man's religion means that God is loyal to the man who loves and serves him. In this

---

[10] Gen. 39:2a.

kind of practical sermon, while the warp comes from the pages in Genesis, the woof is from the life of the businessman in the parish today.

DRAMATIC POWER

The worthy biographical sermon is popular, also, because it appeals to the imagination. The facts themselves are dramatic, and the sermon should accord with the facts. But a little investigation will show that many biographical sermons, so called, are far from dramatic. For instance, one may begin with the prosaic subject, "Esau's Sad Mistake," as though any intelligent layman would care to cross the street to hear about that! What does he care about Esau and Esau's sad mistake? One may spend the first few precious minutes telling the story. In the telling one may make two or three detours, so as to look at similar characters and events, past and present. Thus at the start one complicates a situation which in itself is simple. The "sermon" as a whole may be like the wrong sort of Sunday school lesson—a superficial running commentary on successive verses about Esau.[11] Such a sermon is a "sad mistake." It misrepresents the facts. A dramatic passage calls for a dramatic sermon.

If a sermon is to be dramatic, it makes a vast deal of difference how one starts. At Princeton University chapel on a Sunday morning, the late Sparhawk Jones, of Philadelphia, began by repeating his text, slowly and emphatically: "Is thy servant a dog, that he should do this great thing?"[12] Then there was a pause, while every eye was fixed on the

---

[11] Gen. 25:27-34; cf. Gen. 27.
[12] II Kings 8:13a.

preacher. At length he said, slowly and distinctly, "Dog or no dog, he did it!" After that, he had only to preach. In a dramatic fashion which accorded with the facts he made clear what the man had done in the olden day, and what difference these facts should make in the life of the hearer now. In another striking sermon, of special interest to every man who is young in heart, Clarence E. Macartney preaches from this same text. The subject is, "Your Unknown Self." At the close one may not remember all the facts about the man in the Old Testament story, but one sees as never before that one must rely upon God, not upon self.

The arrangement of the materials is likewise important. In this respect one can learn much from the writer in a popular magazine. For example, if he were dealing with the life of Michael Pupin, the immigrant lad who became a brilliant inventor, as well as a professor at Columbia University, the writer would begin with a sentence or two of vivid contrast between the hero's boyhood in Hungary and his later achievements in his adopted land. This first paragraph would lead up to a key sentence, preferably in the exact words of the hero. This sentence would tell the secret of the transformation. The rest of the article would unfold the truth wrapped up in the sentence. For an object lesson of such technique on a larger scale, see the biography of Calvin Coolidge, *A Puritan in Babylon*.[13] A biographical sermon, after all, is only a popular treatment of facts about a character in the Bible. Hence the minister should study the art of biography.

Still more important is it to have a high spiritual purpose. For instance, sixty years ago when Scotch immigrants were

---

[13] By William Allen White, Macmillan, 1938.

streaming into Western Canada, they used to stop en route at the immigration sheds in Winnepeg. Among them on a certain "Sabbath Day" were a young Scotch farmer and his wife, with their two little sons. As the young parents thought about faring forth into what seemed to them a God-forsaken land, they wished that they had never left their distant home. But then they heard a sermon about "Faith as a Journey into the Unknown." The text was familiar: "By faith . . . . he went out, not knowing whither." [14] The preacher quickly made these familiar words seem new and strange. He was James Robertson, founder of churches in Western Canada. He told the group of homesick strangers that the God who had guided each of them thus far on the pilgrimage of faith would be with him to the journey's end, and bless him as God alone can bless. Long afterward, in a prosperous farm-stead much further west, the minister learned that throughout years of hardship and struggle his sermon had been to the household a sort of guiding star. At the journey's end each of those pilgrims had found God.

After one has learned how to prepare this sort of sermon, one may deal with such a perplexing character as Balaam. In the history of our art almost every English-speaking preacher of note has tried his hand on this baffling personality. These topics show how different artists can look at the same facts and put them together in various ways, each of them helpful: F. W. Robertson, "Perversion" and "Selfishness"; John H. Newman, "Obedience without Love"; Phillips Brooks, "Whole Views of Life"; Marcus Dods, "Compromise and

---

[14] Heb. 11:8b. *The Life of James Robertson,* by Charles W. Gordon (Ralph Connor); Toronto, 1908, pp. 150-52.

Conscience"; T. T. Munger, "The Defeat of Life"; Hugh Black, "Permission without Sanction"; and Charles R. Brown, "The Man Who Plays Fast and Loose." Any such sermon will illustrate the preacher's use of the imagination in applying biblical facts to the everyday needs of the man in the pew.

PRACTICAL USES

The biographical sermon lends itself to various uses. One of them is in preaching doctrine. For example, think about the Providence of God in the life of a busy man. Instead of arguing about the matter, or trying to prove it by logic, one may begin with Joseph.[15] One points out that during his early trials and disappointments, as well as during his adventures in high government office, God was looking out for his servant and friend. This is exactly what Providence means, in so far as it concerns one man. According to the root idea of the word, Providence means that God is the Good Provider. He looks ahead and prepares the way for the man who trusts in him. This is what scholars sometimes call the doctrine of Particular Providence.

Ever since the outbreak of the first World War in 1914, many a strong man has found it difficult to believe this high teaching of the Church. In Toronto not long after the sinking of the "Titanic," a layman heard his pastor preaching about this doctrine of individual Providence.[16] When next the two men met, the layman said to the minister, "I don't believe that the Lord had much if anything to do with it." "Nevertheless," was the reply, "if you had been on board, or

---

[15] Gen. 50:20; cf. Gen. 45:5-8, Rom. 8:28.
[16] See *The Grand Adventure*, sermons by Robert Law, Doran, 1916, pp. 137-48.

if your wife or child had been on board, you would have wished to feel that the Lord had everything to do with it." "I believe you're right," said the layman.

The facts about the life of Joseph, according to the will of God, suggest another sermon about "God's Plan for One's Life." How can one be free while God is in control? Instead of arguing about the matter, as our fathers used to do, one should frankly recognize the mystery, and not try to explain it away. The mystery caused, the writer many sleepless nights when he was a lad of high school age. He would have rejoiced to hear a simple message about Joseph and his brothers as they were all in the hands of God. The four sorts of evil which they committed against their younger brother were like the four sorts of sin which crucified our Lord: envy, greed, lying, murder (in their hearts). For all that evil Joseph's brothers were responsible. Still he could say: "It was not you that sent we hither, but God." What a practical philosophy of the good man's life!

Another doctrine, still closer to the heart of our holy faith, is "The Forgiveness of Sins." Here again one need not argue, and one cannot prove. But one can discuss the practical meaning of sin as a fact in every man's experience, and the practical meaning of forgiveness as being restored to right relations with God. Instead of preaching about sin and pardon as pale, gray abstractions, one may turn to King David as a living object lesson. His experience with Bathsheba shows that sin is a man's way of putting himself out of right relations with God, and that forgiveness is God's way of bringing a sinful human being into right relations. In fact, one may have three successive sermons, with three related texts,[17] as they throw light upon the way in which a conscience-stricken mortal gets right with God. Whoever wrote each of these texts must have known God, for these words voice the feelings of the heart which has found pardon and peace. These are the subjects: "The Cry of Conscience," "The Cry of the Broken Heart," and "The Song of the Forgiven Soul."

A second use of the doctrinal sermon is in preaching about personal ethics. The facts concerning Joseph [18] suggest a sermon about "The Forgiveness of Wrongs." The difference between wrongs and sins is that one commits a wrong against a human being, whereas one commits a sin against God. The principle underlying the sermon is that a man's forgiveness of wrongs ought to be like God's forgiveness of a man's sins. God's forgiveness is full; it is free; it is forever. But the person who has done the wrong must be willing to receive the proffered pardon. Instead of going into these matters abstractly, however, one can bring them out in a popular sermon which shows the great heart of Joseph. In this respect, as in others, he was much like the Lord Jesus.

Another man who forgave deadly wrongs was David.[19] Twice when King Saul was doing his utmost to kill him, young David forgave the king and refrained from taking the king's life. By using a concrete case one can make clear the fact that forgiveness is a sign of strength, and that a forgiving spirit is the surest proof of a man's godliness. After a ruling elder had heard such a message he wrote a tearful letter to the daughter whom he had driven from his door because she had

---

[17] II Sam. 12:1-23; Ps. 51; Ps. 32.
[18] Gen. 45:5-8; 50:20.
[19] I Sam. 24, 26.

married against his will. He asked her to forgive him, and he enclosed money enough to pay her railroad fare home. The next Sunday he proudly introduced her to the minister. That sermon had brought the father the sort of peace which comes through being right with God and with the person whom one has wronged. According to the most widely heard minister of our day, Harry Emerson Fosdick, the test of an ethical sermon is the number of requests for personal interviews concerning how to do the will of God as revealed in the sermon.

A third use of the biographical sermon is in preaching social ethics; for instance, a man's duty to the state. This sort of sermon is not in favor with some of our best people. But since there is in the Bible a good deal about such matters, Christian people should not object to what one preaches from the Book. The obvious way to deal with any such subject concretely is to single out some public character in Hebrew history. In a day when we all are thinking about dictators in Europe, and about the need for wise rulers here at home, there is a call for preaching about "The Biblical Ideal of Leadership." The text may be the words of the wise old men to the silly young king Rehoboam: "If thou wilt be a servant unto this people this day, and wilt serve them, and answer them, and speak good words to them, then they will be thy servants for ever." [20] But, alas, the present-day leader, like that silly young king, may not hearken to the words of the wise men. They have witnessed the folly wrought by extravagance and oppression in high places. They fear that the body politic will fall to pieces. Now as then, the call is

---

[20] I Kings 12:7.

for the ruler who will look upon himself as the servant of God and God's people. As Grover Cleveland used to insist, "Public office is a sacred trust."

YOUNG PEOPLE'S NEEDS

Other uses of the biographical sermon have to do with preaching to young people. They need guidance, for example, in matters relating to courtship and marriage. As a rule one prefers to take up the subject at the evening service, when the little boys and girls ought to be at home in bed. Without stooping to sensationalism, or to sentimentality, one can present the biblical ideals concerning marriage and the home. For the text one may turn to Genesis. It is no accident that the first book in the Bible, and one of the greatest, is about God and the home.[21] In this book the facts about the long-distance courtship of Isaac and Rebecca may lead to a sermon about "A Marriage Made in Heaven."[22] While such a way of finding a wife would not appeal to any young man now, the principles which emerge in the fascinating record should still prevail. Throughout the sermon, as throughout the biblical account, the emphasis is upon the personal leadership of God.

When God has his way in the founding of a home, two broad principles are clear. First, the plans for the marriage are made in heaven. In his own good time and way, the Lord brings together the two that he intends for each other. They should belong to the same race, and occupy much the same station in life. In the eyes of God a young Japanese man or

---

[21] See "Religion in the Home," in *Bible History: Genesis to Esther,* by Andrew W. Blackwood, Revell, 1928, pp. 9-33.
[22] Gen. 24.

woman is as good as any of our sons or daughters, but still we cannot look with favor upon interracial marriage. In that sort of union the children suffer. Likewise should the husband and the wife live on much the same level of culture. Only in the fairy tale does the charming prince marry the daughter of the beggar and live with her in continued bliss. Above all, the husband and the wife should believe in the same God, and love to worship at the same church. These are some of the details in the plans which God makes for the marriage which he is waiting to bless.

Thus the first line of thought has to do with the biblical ideal of marriage. It is the most beautiful of life's opening doors. This line of thought appears again and again in the preaching of the minister who appeals to young people. Once in a while there is an entire sermon holding up the ideal of marriage in the light of heaven.[23] In such a sermon the second main part stands out in bold contrast, for the emphasis here is practical. The plans made in heaven must be carried out on earth. Even the noblest husband and the most charming wife are as human—and they may be as different temperamentally—as Isaac and Rebecca. They must live and love, as well as work and suffer, in the midst of human limitations.[24] In preaching about these mundane matters it would be easy to become facetious. But surely it is better to speak of marriage as almost a sacrament. Preach up, not down! The ideal is that love should lead to wedlock. If the love is Christian on both sides, it will enable husband and wife to live together until death parts them. If there were more teaching

---

[23] For other sermon texts see Eph. 5:25-27; Rev. 21:2; Isa. 62:5.
[24] Cf. *What Men Live By,* by Richard C. Cabot, M.D., Boston, 1914.

of this sort in pulpit and home, there might be less need for preaching about divorce.

In the preceding paragraphs, every statement of fact—except for the local color—is suggested by the chapter about the courtship and marriage of Isaac and Rebecca. The statements are all in the present tense, because one is preaching a present-day sermon, and not explaining a passage in the Old Testament. A little earlier in the hour one has read the entire chapter. It repeats the main ideas so often that before the end of the reading even the least alert hearer is familiar with the facts, as they have to do chiefly with the will of God.

The chapter is long. If the evening order of worship does not allow time for such a long lesson, why not quit at the end of verse thirty-one, and then read the rest of the chapter immediately before the sermon? How could one employ those few precious minutes with more pleasure and profit to the young man and woman who have stolen into the rear pew, where they may be holding hands? In such a popular interpretation of a passage in the Bible—as Mark Twain once said about explaining a poem by Robert Browning—the rule is simply to read it, provided one knows how to read. As for the sermon, especially in preaching to young people, one keeps largely to the present tense.

The biographical sermon likewise lends itself to preaching at commencement time. Toward the end of his days in school a young man ought to be thinking about "Life's Great Permanent Choices." They are usually three, though they ought to be four. First, "Whom shall I serve, God or myself?" Second, "What shall I do with my life? Shall I teach, or farm, or become a minister?" Third, "Whom shall I wed? A daughter of the King or a child of the world?" Fourth, "Where shall we live? Where we can do most good, or where we can get most gold?" For the text one may turn to the record about Lot.[25] He yielded to selfish motives. He chose to move toward Sodom. Soon he was living in that city, which was a cesspool of sin. Ere long Sodom was in Lot. Though he was saved, it was as by fire. These facts are a sort of parable in action. They should lead to a dramatic, gripping message. "Choose well! Your choice is brief, yet endless." In any such sermon, however dramatic, the emphasis should be upon God, not upon Lot.

In a state agricultural college one of the seniors was talking about the baccalaureate sermon: "For once in their lives our professors all listened to a sermon! The strange parson advised each of us to do three things: first, accept Christ and join the church; second, marry the girl who is sure to be a good mother; third, settle down on a farm here in Mississippi." Of course it is not every young man's duty to spend all his days back on the old home farm, but it is every young man's privilege to ascertain the will of God, and then do his holy will as it is done in heaven.

At a college for women the sermon would be different. If they have specialized in domestic science they should be glad to hear about themselves as "Daughters of Martha." In a school of another sort, where the emphasis is upon the fine arts, the sermon may be about "Daughters of Mary." In each case the underlying facts are the same. Jesus loved Martha, as well as Mary, and their brother Lazarus. In the three passages where the sisters appear together in the presence of the

[25] Gen. 13:11.

Lord Jesus,[26] the records show how he brings a blessing in the hour of joy, in the hour of grief, and in the hour of service. While it may not prove easy to make the sermon interesting to strange young women who are not accustomed to biblical preaching, perhaps the novelty will attract their attention and the helpfulness of the sermon appeal to their hearts. Many of our young people are more thoughtful than we ministers suppose.

OTHER PREACHING VALUES

Time would fail one even to mention the other uses of the biographical sermon. For example, it lends itself admirably to the needs of a special occasion. It may be some anniversary in the local church. Since the people are looking backward, they should be mentally prepared for a message about a well-known biblical character—it may be Elijah. The occasion calls for a text which is brief and easy to remember. If it contains a figure which one can make clear and luminous, this helps in appealing to the imagination. Here is such a text: "He took up the mantle of Elijah." [27] In the surrounding verses one finds that Elisha had asked for a double portion of Elijah's spirit, and that the younger man was to receive that double portion when he took up the mantle of Elijah. In the Hebrew household the double portion was that of the eldest son, whose social obligations were doubly great. The resulting sermon is about "The Mantle of the Godly Father."

In a sermon for a special occasion the opening words have to do with the occasion. Especially in preaching to strangers,

---

[26] Luke 10:38-42; John 11:18-29; 12:1-3.
[27] II Kings 2:13a; cf. 2:15b.

it may be necessary to attract attention, not to say good will. As soon as possible, one should lead them to think about the purpose of the hour, which has to do with servants of God who have fallen asleep. Thus one fixes attention upon Elijah. In the first main part of the sermon one speaks about his mantle, which is the symbol of service. One may speak about the mantle of the prophet, the mantle of the reformer, the mantle of the saint. In this use of the term, a saint is notable for strength and courage in doing the will of God amid a hostile world. Throughout this first main part of the message, the emphasis is upon the service of God and men.

The more important and difficult part has to do with the spirit of God's servant, the spirit of loyalty. According to a popular book of philosophy [28]—a book which every minister should inwardly digest—loyalty is the willing, practical, thoroughgoing devotion of a person to a cause as that cause is embodied in a person. Elijah was a mighty servant of the common good because at heart he was ever loyal. The cause to which he was loyal was the Kingdom, and the person was God. In modern terms the call is for loyalty to the Kingdom, loyalty to Christ, and loyalty to the Church. In the light of the sermon the man in the pew ought to bow down and pray, "O Lord, let me take up the mantle of my sainted father, and let me have a double portion of his spirit."

Sometimes the facts within the parish call for a different kind of special sermon. Recently at the First Presbyterian Church of Germantown, Pennsylvania, when the people were praying for the coming of a young minister to take the place of the one who had been their leader for years before he went

---

[28] *The Philosophy of Loyalty,* by Josiah Royce, Macmillan, 1908.

home to God, the visiting preacher spoke about Apollos.[29] The message about this eloquent preacher in the Bible led one of the hearers to think gratefully about his own boyhood pastor. The layman had the sermon printed for free distribution. The subject is, "A Minister Marked for Distinction." Perhaps one should report that the people soon called this sort of young interpreter. In the sermon, which doubtless helped to lead them aright, these are the main affirmations:

1. He is eloquent, but accurate.
2. He is cultured, but ardent.
3. He is dogmatic, but docile.
4. He is evangelistic, but educational.

---

[29] Acts 18:24-28.

THE BIOGRAPHICAL SERIES

WHEN the minister has tasted the joys of preaching a number of biographical sermons he begins to ask himself, "Why not have a series?" If there are two services on the Lord's Day, the series will usually come at the second service. Attendance at morning worship is largely a matter of habit; but if the people come out for the second service, which may be vespers, there is evidently a strong attraction. One of the best ways to attract them is to plan a series of biographical sermons. After an interval there may be another series, usually of a different sort, perhaps doctrinal.

In every series there should be a unifying title. The various sermons should follow an order which will insure both progress and climax. In a biographical series the order is usually that of time; thus one plans to keep the mind of the hearer moving forward. In discussing the biographical series we shall first think about successive sermons which deal with various characters, more or less alike; and then about sermons which have to do with a single character. Afterwards we shall think about the still more vital subject, how to prepare a popular series of biographical sermons.

ABOUT RELATED CHARACTERS

A good place to find material for a series about related characters is Genesis. In Genesis the obvious place to begin is with Abraham. Since the opening sermon is to be about a man whose name means "exalted father," and whose chief distinction was faith, the topic of the sermon may be, "The Faith of a Godly Father." As every student of the Bible is aware, faith shines out in various ways. Sometimes the emphasis is upon saving faith; again, there is seeing faith. There may be serving faith; or the stress may be upon suffering faith—that is, the faith of the man who suffers without sin. In the sermon about Abraham, and throughout the series, the emphasis is upon serving faith.[1] Serving faith means doing the will of God, day after day, gladly and well, not because one knows why, but because one trusts God. With some such key sentence one looks at faith from three successive points of view, each suggested by the experiences of Abraham. Faith means—

Courage to start doing the will of God.
Perseverance to keep on doing the will of God.
Willingness to make the supreme sacrifice, according to the
will of God.

The second sermon may be about Isaac, or rather about his God. The topic here is "The God of the Average Man." [2] Isaac was always second to somebody else. He was his mother's son, his wife's husband, his son's father. He might have posed as "the forgotten man." He was the sort of peace-loving neighbor about whom people laugh when they see the comic strip, "Bringing Up Father." They say about such a man, "He never will set the world on fire!" Probably not, but who wishes to have the world set on fire? If there were more men like this gentle lover of peace, there would be

[1] Heb. 11:8b.
[2] Gen. 26:25.

fewer wars and strikes. Under God, the welfare of our world depends largely upon the average man. As Lincoln used to say, the Lord must love the common people; he has made so many of them.

Here we are, thinking about Isaac, when we should be thinking about his God. The facts about this inconspicuous, unspectacular, two-talent man are of vital moment to us, because they show how deeply God is concerned about the average man, from his conception in the womb to his burial in the grave. This is the sort of man whom God delights to bless. In the body of the sermon one shows that God blesses the average man in three different ways: in his own heart, in his dealings with his fellow-men, and most of all through his children. Through the direct descendants of Isaac, God caused the books of the Bible to be written, the Hebrew and the Christian Church to be founded, and the Kingdom to be established on earth. According to the flesh, the Lord Jesus came from the seed of Isaac.

After a sermon about the God of Isaac, a lay officer said to his pastor: "I wish you would preach about the God of Jacob; most of us laymen are more like him than we are like his father." The resulting sermon about Jacob dealt with the best thing we know about God. The subject was, "The God of the Wicked Man." [3] Here again the line of thought was threefold.

First, think about the goodness of God—perhaps one might say the courage of God—in choosing such a wicked man as Jacob. At home he had deceived his poor old blind father. Jacob had likewise cheated his twin brother. In the far

---

[3] Gen. 28:10-22, especially verse 15.

76

country Jacob had cheated his father-in-law and business partner, who had begun by cheating Jacob. Surely this man deserved his name, which means "Supplanter." And yet God chose Jacob to be his personal representative!

Second, think about the perseverance of God in blessing such a bad man throughout the middle years of life. God blessed him in his business and in his home. If one asks how God can be patient with a man who keeps sinning against his fellows, perhaps the reply is that if God never blessed a man who is imperfect there would be no hope for any of us. The chief way in which he blesses, however, is often through conscience, which will not give one peace until one is right with God and man.

Third, and best of all, think about the grace of God in transforming the heart and the life of a man who is no longer young.[4] Sometimes we forget that God is able to change the soul of a man in the middle years of life, and that he is able to work the transformation in a single night. Of course God had been preparing the way for years, but the change was sudden. After the change of Jacob's heart at Peniel,[5] he seems never again to have stooped to his old tricky ways. So complete was the transformation that henceforth he had to bear a new name, Israel, which means, "One who perseveres with God." Another topic for this sermon about the God of Jacob would be "The Gospel in the Old Testament."

In a series lasting through the month the closing sermon may be about the God of Joseph, under the heading, "The God of the Normal Man," or perhaps, "The Religion of Healthy-

---

[4] See "The Everlasting Mercy," by John Masefield, *Poems*, Macmillan, 1935.
[5] Gen. 32:24-32.

Mindedness." The thought underlying the whole series is that made famous by William James in his *Varieties of Religious Experience*.[6] The four sermons have to do with four prominent characters, who represent four different types of men. These types are in every parish. For example, a young man might say after the series: "My grandfather is like austere Abraham; my father is like easygoing Isaac; my uncle resembles dynamic Jacob; my brother resembles lovable Joseph. Like those Old Testament worthies, my people too love God." Thus a good series tends to exalt the God who makes himself known through the experience of men like those in the pews.

What shall one entitle the series? The best time to bestow the all-inclusive name is after the separate sermons are fairly well in hand. Since the emphasis throughout is upon "The Faith of Our Fathers," that may be the general title. From a slightly different point of view, one may prefer "The God of Every Man." In the neat little folder announcing the series one may print the following words from Pascal. When he died in 1622 his friends found sewed up in his doublet a piece of paper which he had written: "God of Abraham, God of Isaac, God of Jacob—not of philosophers and savants—God of Jesus Christ. Thy God and my God; thy God shall be my God." In preparing each of the four messages this should be the minister's ideal: "Let me so preach that my hearer will resolve in his heart to do the will of God as revealed in this sermon."

The experienced preacher may wish to start out on a more difficult trail. If he is appealing to men and women of

---

[6] Longmans, Green, 1928.

refinement, as in a college community, he may prepare a series about "Practical Idealists of the Bible." A practical idealist is a man whose life and work from day to day are determined by the vision which has come to him from God. The following is a partial list of men who were both dreamers of dreams and doers of deeds: Jacob, Joseph, Moses, Gideon, David, Isaiah, Daniel. In such a series, as a rule, one keeps to the same Testament. But the closing sermon may well be about Christ, not in the sense that he belongs with the heroes of the faith, but that he alone embodies the ideals toward which they strove. A sermon about Christ as the Ideal Man would be fitting in a series which reached its climax two or three weeks before Christmas.

If some of the same characters appear in the present series as in the last one, or in the one a year earlier, this repetition may show that the pastor is a skillful teacher. He may turn to Jacob or to Joseph again and again, each time from a different point of view and for a different purpose. The popular preacher looks upon the typical church-goer as a hero worshiper. Throughout the sermon on Joseph the hero seems to represent the layman himself, as he is in his dreams. In order to preach the series, the minister must be a Christian idealist. Christian idealism in the pulpit is contagious. So is the lack of idealism. Would that every man who comes to church, especially while young, might there be exposed to lofty Christian idealism!

During the weeks prior to an important election one may have a series about "Statesmen of the Bible." Here again every pastor should make his own list, according to his personal interests and his sense of values. To the selection of the characters and to the singling out of the texts he should devote much care. In the list as it appears on paper—both in the bulletin and on a card for distribution through the Men's Bible Class—there should be nothing to reveal the identity of any character, or the location of any text. Rather should there be a frank appeal to curiosity. The rule is to put on the paper as little as possible, provided the copy is clear and inviting.

The following list is from the trial work sheet of a pastor who has formed the habit of mulling over a series at odd moments for several months before he lets it assume the final shape: Joseph (Gen. 41:38), Moses (Deut. 34:10), David (I Sam. 16:7), Solomon (I Kings 3:9), Hezekiah (Isa. 37:14), Nehemiah (Neh. 6:3), Daniel (Dan. 6:5), with a climactic message about Christ as the ideal King (Isa. 32:1, 2). The list is too long, but that is an advantage. It is easier to omit a character here and another there than it would be to fill up a vacant place. The theory is that of the athletic coach who will keep the most spectacular player on the bench in order to win the game.

In a series the temptation is to stress the negative, not the positive. In Toronto recently a strong pulpit expositor had a successful series of ten sermons about "Bible Types of Modern Failures." In a series this long one may work over into the New Testament and thus include Judas. This sort of negative preaching is likely to prove popular, because the evil immediately attracts attention. Then too the average preacher seems to know more about sin than about holiness. Perhaps this is why the most skillfully delineated character, and the most popular, in *Paradise Lost* is Satan, not Christ. Nevertheless, God surely prefers to make himself known through the sermon about the man who is true, not the one who is false. Like his Lord, the Christian herald of the Good News should become known primarily for what Thomas Carlyle calls "The Everlasting Yea."

ABOUT ONE CHARACTER

Thus far we have had in view the series about a number of characters more or less alike. This kind of series is relatively easy to prepare. But when one becomes well acquainted with Elijah or Daniel, one longs to tarry with him for a while. A series about any spiritual giant may be difficult to plan. But if one knows how, and then works hard, the resulting sermons are more likely to prove effective than if one painted each time a different person. At Westminster Chapel in London Harris E. Kirk preached one summer for ten successive Sunday evenings about Jacob, the next summer about David, the third summer about Moses. On a Sunday evening in July, when a visitor from the States dropped in at the church thirty minutes before the hour for the service, the people were already assembling. They were eager to hear another of what one of them called "those thoughtful sermons from the Bible."

During the summer, when people are longing to fly away to the hills, one may have a series of five sermons about Moses, or rather about God. The subject is, "With God among the Mountains." Another series is, "With Christ among the Mountains." As in the earthly life of our Lord, there are in the experience of Moses five mountain scenes. They show how God leads the man who is finding his way, step by step,

81

in doing the will of the Heavenly Father. This may be the organizing principle of the series. Otherwise the temptation will be to turn aside from religion proper and try to teach history or geography. What the man in the pew needs to learn is about these five pivotal experiences in the life of one whom God called to heroic service.

Let us glance at the five sermons. Beginning at the burning bush, one may preach successively about "The Soul's Discovery of God," [7] "The Majesty of God's Holy Law," [8] "The Meaning of the Intercessory Prayer," [9] "The Blessedness of the Unknown Future," [10] and "The Old Testament Preparation for Christ." [11] None of these passages is easy to interpret. But if one tarries in each mountain long enough to feel at home with Moses and his God, one can help the hearer to see that even the greatest man in the Old Testament was great only in the hands of God. Would that in every high place now there were a man like Moses! The secret of such greatness lies in the soul's discovery of God.

> "Earth's crammed with heaven,
>   And every common bush afire with God;
>   But only he who sees takes off his shoes,
>   The rest sit round and pick blackberries." [12]

Still more dramatic should be a series about Elijah. Why was it Elijah, rather than Isaiah, or Hosea, who appeared with Moses on the Mount of Transfiguration? In the eyes of the Hebrews, who surely knew their heroes, Elijah was the

---

[7] Exod. 3:5.
[8] Exod. 19:3.
[9] Exod. 34:2.
[10] Deut. 32:52.
[11] Matt. 17:3.
[12] *Aurora Leigh*, by Elizabeth Barrett Browning.

greatest of the prophets. To us he may not seem so great as others, because he did not write. Mistakenly we think of a prophet as chiefly a man of words, whereas he was primarily a man of deeds. From the biblical point of view, who among the seers towered higher than this man of God? In the brief records about Elijah, "the prophet of fire," there are six dramatic scenes. Most of them are among the mountains. Thus there is an opening for six dramatic sermons. The general heading may be, "A Strong Man's Religion."

The topic of the first sermon may be, "God's Care in Hard Times." [13] While living by the brook, as many a strong man has been forced to live of late, the future prophet learned to depend upon God. When the brook dried up, as many a man's only means of livelihood has failed in recent years, the Lord led his servant to the home of a widow who was facing starvation. There he learned to sympathize with the woes of God's suffering poor. Thus the future prophet learned to depend on God and to have sympathy for the helpless. What a postgraduate course in pastoral theology!

The second sermon may be about "God's Will for Our Nation." [14] This is probably the most dramatic scene in Old Testament history. Then, as now, the forces of secularism were mighty. For a while on Mount Carmel, as among the French after the Revolution, and in Russia a hundred years later, the issue between God and Anti-God seemed to hang in the balance. But through the leadership of Elijah, God won the day. If we had such a leader now, we might have in our nation a revival of old-fashioned right-

---

[13] I Kings 17.
[14] I Kings 18.

eousness. Meanwhile the temptation of the preacher is to speak heatedly about the present crisis in Europe or Asia, and to forget that there is likewise peril here at home. A more subtle temptation is to prate about secular politics, and not preach about God.

The third topic is "God's Cure for the Blues."[15] The mightiest man of his day was decidedly human. He became so blue that he wished to die. He found God's cure while on a midsummer holiday. This strong man, who had temporarily lost his grip, visited in turn two distant places where his fathers had come close to God. Often it is easy to feel conscious of God's nearness back on the old farm where the fathers found him day after day. Amid those ancestral scenes the weary servant of God found rest and food, with a complete change of thought and feeling. Ere long he gained a sense of God's presence, not in "the earthquake, wind, and fire," but in the voice of gentle stillness. Our God is unspectacular. He can shout, but he prefers to whisper. When he restores to spiritual health the soul which is sick and willing for death, God sends his servant back to his home and his work, a humbler and a stronger man.

The fourth message is about "God's Voice to the Conscience."[16] Among the biographical sermons thus far, no one has been so difficult to prepare and to preach as this one about the conscience of the layman. It is always hard to preach about personal duty and personal sin. It is easy to declaim against the sins of a man who lived long ago, or of one who lives far away now. But when the minister appeals

---

[15] I Kings 19.
[16] I Kings 21, especially verse 20c.

to the conscience of the man in the pew, that man hears the voice of God speaking directly to him about his own sins. Such a sermon calls for ministerial courage, which is another name for faith in God. "Thou hast sold thyself to work evil in the sight of the Lord." What a way to speak to one's king! If there were more preaching of this sort in the pulpit today, there would be more iron in the blood of the man in the pew. There might also be a larger number of men at the public worship of God.

The next sermon in the series is about "God's Choice of a New Leader." [17] The last message is about "God's Approval of Christ." This is where the strong man's religion finds its center and its glory. Just as Moses and Elijah were present in spirit on the Mount of Transfiguration because the Lord Jesus was there, so does the modern man at church wish to come face to face with the Living Christ and to hear the Heavenly Father say, "This is my beloved Son, in whom I am well pleased." Thus the series may close with a sermon about the glory of God in the hour of worship. [18]

FOR DAYS OF UPHEAVAL

In a time of world chaos and ruin there is need for a series from the Book of Daniel. The first half affords abundance of material for six successive sermons. The latter half is so difficult that one may leave it until later, when one may have more biblical insight, as well as homiletical skill. But the first six chapters present no insuperable difficulties, provided one is willing to preach the facts as they stand. The aim is

[17] II Kings 2:1-14.
[18] Matt. 17:3-5.

to preach the truth as revealed to the modern man through this timely book, and not to discuss the facts about the book itself.

It is possible to preach from the first part of the book in one of three different ways. During any year it is wise to preach only a single series about Daniel, but if conditions throughout the world continue to be chaotic, one may return to the book in three successive years and preach about it from three different points of view. When the people of God have their backs to the wall, they can never hear too much about the God of Daniel. "Our God is able!" Among all our other needs, the chief need of the world and the individual today is the discovery of God and the acceptance of his holy will.[19]

The easiest way to approach these chapters is to watch for what they teach concerning "The Power of a Man's Religion." The purpose is to lead the layman to trust God during days when world conditions threaten to overwhelm faith. In each sermon there is a text, or key verse, which unlocks the gateway into a fertile field. These are the topics. First, "The Glory of a Young Man's Conscience."[20] This sermon permits one to exalt the habit of temperance, or self-control. Second, "The Heart of a Strong Man's Creed."[21] This message, the most difficult of the six to prepare, is about making God the Absolute Monarch in one's life and world. Third, "The Power to Save from the Fire."[22] Here sounds forth the triumphant assurance, "Our God, whom we serve,

---

[19] Cf. *The Faith We Declare,* by Edwin Lewis, Cokesbury, 1939.
[20] Dan. 1:8.
[21] Dan. 2:44.
[22] Dan. 3:17, 18.

is able to deliver." What a cry of victory! For another shout of exultation, listen to Martin Luther's battle song of the Reformation, "Ein' feste Burg ist unser Gott!"

Fourth, "The Transformation of the Dictator." [23] Here one stresses the refrain which rings forth from the chapter again and again, "Till thou know that the Most High ruleth in the kingdom of men, and giveth it to whomsoever he will." Why not pray that such a transforming experience may come to more than one dictator in Europe or Asia? Sometimes we pray for "a tyrant's downfall," but these are scarcely the words to use in public prayer. According to the Book of Daniel, even the most ruthless dictator is a sinful human being, whom the grace of God is able to transform.

The fifth sermon may be about "The Weight of a Man's Soul"; [24] and the sixth, "The Power of a Man's God." [25] Here again sounds forth the question which reaches to the very center of a man's religion, "Is thy God, whom thou servest continually, able to deliver thee from the lions?" The sermon is the answer.

In a more difficult series one can use these chapters as the basis for six sermons about the problems of present-day society. That was the trail once marked out by Robert J. McMullen, a missionary and educational leader in China. He was thinking about the needs of his adopted land before the invasion by Japan. His subject was, "Safeguards against Six National Perils." Any thoughtful minister can prepare a similar series about the social problems of our land today. In each topic the stress is upon the safeguard, not the peril:

[23] Dan. 4:25b.
[24] Dan. 5:27.
[25] Dan. 6:20.

Luxurious Living .... Biblical Simplicity
Material Prosperity .... Superiority of the Spiritual
Religious Opportunism .... Religious Convictions
Self-Glorification .... Recognition of God's Rule
Widespread Irreverence .... Fear of the Lord
Selfish Ambition .... Quiet Trust in God

Most difficult of all is the series where the emphasis is upon the biblical teachings about God. The purpose here is to show how the truth concerning God ministers to the daily needs of man. As Phillips Brooks says, "Preach doctrine, preach all the doctrine that you know, and learn forever more and more; but preach it always, not that men may believe it, but that men may be saved by believing it." [26] In this series the general subject may be, "With God in Days of Peril."

In a certain parish the visiting minister preached the following sermons on six consecutive Sunday evenings, which included the Christmas season:

> With God on Life's Proving Ground
> With God before the Dictator
> With God in the Fiery Furnace
> With God as King of Kings
> With God at the Godless Feast
> With God in the Lion's Den

The message about the King of Kings fell on Christmas Eve. The sermon about the godless feast was on New Year's Eve, in a year when the *New York Times* said that it required a thousand special policemen to control the revelers in Times Square. The message about praying in the lion's den came just before the Week of Prayer. Hence the series proved to be timely. Ordinarily, however, the local pastor would have

[26] *Lectures on Preaching,* E. P. Dutton, 1877, p. 129.

the series during the autumn, and do something else at the holiday season.

HOW TO PREPARE A SERIES

Every minister should work in his own way. Likewise should one proceed differently in each series, according to the controlling purpose. However, it should be possible for the young minister to learn from the disheartening experiences of one who in his early days had to work by the old-fashioned method of trial and error. It would have been more pleasant for him and more profitable for his people if he could have followed a trail blazed out by some earlier pioneer.

First, as in planning a book, one decides upon the controlling purpose. One may even give the series a tentative name, though that usually emerges later. When the pastor knows his people, and loves them dearly, he should ask himself in his study: "What do they need most at this season of the year?" When once the controlling purpose is clearly in view, it should guide and restrain him, both in mapping out the series as a whole, and in preparing each sermon. This is what one may call purposeful planning.

If there were no unifying purpose, there would be a series only in name. If the minister were aiming at nothing, he would hit it every time. The aimless pulpit ranter might as well be shooting arrows into the air. But the man who works hard on a series is likely to err in a different direction. He may have no practical purpose for the series because he may simply be trying to expound the various passages. He ought to remember that every preaching passage in the Bible was inspired in order that it might minister to some human need.[27] Partly for this reason, the minister who preaches from the Bible ought to know the people before him, personally and well. Otherwise how could he satisfy the hunger of their hearts?

For example, in 1936 the writer preached for five successive Sundays at Birkenhead, England. Without having in view any high, specific purpose, he attempted to use a series. Too late he discovered that in addressing strangers across the sea it would have been better to work from week to week, and then shift the plans according to the increasing light on local needs. In preparing his series he had not looked forward to seeing in the churchyard a stately monument recording the names of thirty-one young men whom that parish had sent out to die during the first World War. Neither had he expected to see in the pews scarcely a man between the ages of forty and sixty, but an unusual number of unmarried women. He found that in almost every home there was at least one vacant chair. He soon learned that what those dear friends needed most was a word of hope from the living God. " 'Comfort ye, comfort ye my people,' saith your God. 'Speak to the heart of Jerusalem, and cry unto her that her warfare is accomplished.' " [28] God bless and shield those dear people now when war has once again loosed her fateful lightnings!

In preparing for a series one's controlling purpose may be ethical, evangelistic, or pastoral. Of course these labels overlap. Judging from the specific sermons, rather than the title, one feels that Clarence E. Macartney's purpose in *The Way*

[27] See II Tim. 3:17. In the Greek the conjunction strongly indicates purpose.
[28] Isa. 40:1, 2a. The rendering is from the Hebrew.

of a Man with a Maid was ethical. The minister was evidently striving to help young people, individually, to solve their problems about courtship and marriage, and to solve them according to the revealed will of God. In another series, *The Truce of God,* the purpose was evangelistic. In a third series, *At the Golden Altar,* the purpose was pastoral. The series had to do with prayer, a subject about which a wise pastor preaches again and again.[29]

On the fourth page of the neat gray folder which announced Macartney's series about prayer, one finds the words of the basic text,[30] with the following explanation: "These seven sermons on prayer will show from the lives of tempted, struggling souls how prayer brings victory and peace." What a purpose!

Again, in the light of the controlling purpose one should plan the series as a whole. In doing so one thinks about the number of sermons, the topics, the order, and the general title. After one has phrased the general title, one revises the phrasing of the specific topics, so that there will be harmony throughout. This kind of planning calls for ability of no mean order. Likewise does it call for work, and that covering a number of weeks. Instead of slaving over the task all one day, and far into the night, it is usually better to begin several weeks or months in advance. Thus one allows time for the plans to mature under the gentle influence of "subconscious incubation." In short, it is safe to assume that the people will remember a series as long after they hear it as the minister

---

[29] See *Lord, Teach Us to Pray,* by Alexander Whyte, Doran, 1923; and *The Lower Levels of Prayer,* by George S. Stewart, Cokesbury, 1940.

[30] Rev. 8:3.

has had it in mind before it starts. It takes more time to raise a crop of wheat than a bed of mushrooms.

As for the number of sermons in the series, there is little uniformity. As in driving a team of horses, the larger the number, the more skill must there be in the driver, partly because each horse is different. Hence it is a bold man who announces a series of more than eight sermons. Ofttimes six would be better, and sometimes four is best. There are advantages in working by the month. If the series is long, instead of increasing climactically from week to week, the interest of the people may begin to sag. As in preaching a sermon, it is better to stop while they are still hungry than to keep on after they wish one to stop. Stop, however, is not the word. A series should lead up, climactically, to the fulfillment of its purpose.

Still further, one should have every sermon ready, in extensive outline, before one makes any announcement. Otherwise there is likely to be a lack of unity, and there may be something approaching a farce. Once when the writer was young he rashly announced a series of four evening sermons about heaven. Then, as now, the people were deeply concerned about what lies beyond the grave. But the young parson did not know enough about the Bible and the needs of human hearts to preach four successive sermons about the heavenly home. On the first evening the response was excellent, on the second satisfactory, on the third poor, on the fourth disappointing. From week to week the preaching grew poorer and the attendance was smaller. The people did their part. The pastor alone was to blame.

If that young parson had used plain horse sense he would

not have announced as his closing message, "The Geography of Heaven." To this day he does not know where God's islands "lift their fronded palms in air." Hence all that he could do was to suggest practical ways for the hearer to help make the home town more like heaven; that is, like the "beautiful isle of somewhere." Even if the hearer needed such a message, he came expecting something else, and he went away feeling that he had been lured into church under false pretenses. In order to prevent a loss of confidence on the part of the layman whom one is trying to reach, one should have the series ready in all its parts, especially the closing sermon.[31] The rule for a series is, plan everything before you announce anything.

Last of all, prepare each sermon as a separate unit. Let it stand squarely on its own feet. The temptation is to devote the first few paragraphs to a bird's-eye view of what has gone before, and the last few paragraphs to a preview of what is to come. But those first few paragraphs will afford a rare opportunity to focus the hearer's attention on the message for the present Sunday evening, and the closing words will afford an ideal opportunity to send him forth resolved to live in the light which has just come from God. In other words, do not look back, or look ahead. Look into the face of the man in the pew, and then preach the truth which will make him free.

---

[31] "In order to make sure of having a good last act, when I wrote *The Admirable Crichton*, I wrote the last act first."—James M. Barrie.

CHAPTER V

THE PREACHING PARAGRAPH

IN preaching from the Bible the most frequent unit is the paragraph. While not every paragraph yields a preaching message, any major book of the Bible affords enough paragraph material for preaching month after month. In fact, there is so much inviting material that in preaching through a book one usually selects what one wishes, and leaves the rest for other times. One learns to look on a preaching paragraph much as a sculptor looks on a waiting block of marble in which he beholds the coming statue. The right sort of paragraph affords all the biblical materials for the coming sermon.

This way of preaching ought to be profitable, for in the Bible the unit of composition is the paragraph. Except in certain sections—notably large parts of Proverbs—the unit of thought is the paragraph. Hence one often studies the American Revised Version, as well as the more recent translations, such as Moffatt's and Goodspeed's. In the pulpit and on other formal occasions one reads from the King James, with its majestic cadences. But in the study one should ever have at hand a version which gives the paragraph its due place in the sun. Better still, one should go back to the Greek and the Hebrew.

For a series of object lessons in preaching from the paragraph, turn to the recent book by Frederick K. Stamm.[1]

---

[1] *The Conversations of Jesus*, Harper, 1939. See pp. 71-77, 158-64.

One of his sermons is on "Jesus and Our Doubts." The biblical basis is a paragraph in which John the Baptist is prominent,[2] though of course the Lord Jesus is the central, dominant figure. Another of these radio sermons is on "The Way to Win a Man."[3] The person whom our Lord wins is Zacchaeus. He is a social outcast because of his business. Any such message is all the more effective when the minister speaks largely in the present tense, and makes the man in the pew see how the truth applies to him personally. In no other way could one preach more helpfully about a strong man's doubts, or about a strong man's conversion. Truly these paragraphs in the Gospels display the "highlights of the Bible."

During the first year or two it may be wise to preach from a chosen paragraph only occasionally, perhaps once a month, and then do something else on the other three Sundays. In old-fashioned expository lecturing one would preach straight through the book; but while one is learning how to preach from the paragraph, one ought to use the method sparingly. Meanwhile one is giving the people an opportunity to become accustomed to this novel sort of diet. At least it may seem new to them. But if one keeps setting the table with abundance of biblical food, well prepared and served warm, the people will get used to one's preaching from the paragraph. Of course the popular appeal of the sermon will depend a good deal on one's homiletical divination in choosing the passage, and much more on one's homiletical skill in preparing the message. It should glow!

---

[2] Matt. 11:2-6.
[3] Luke 19:1-10.

SELECTING THE PARAGRAPH

The choice of the paragraph deserves more attention than it usually receives. The interpreter who lacks experience should select a passage which presents comparatively few difficulties. He may think that Paul was the greatest of Christians, and that Romans is the supreme book in the New Testament. Nevertheless, the novice should wait a few years before he undertakes to prepare a sermon from a paragraph in the eighth chapter of Romans. While that chapter is full of gold, the gold does not lie strewn about on the ground. Another pastor may think highly of the Epistle to the Hebrews, or of the Apocalypse. Even so, that is not a sufficient reason for his rushing into steep mountain country in quest of material for his first paragraph sermon. Even at the expense of seeming childlike, he should select a paragraph which is easy to understand, as well as explain. How then should one make the selection?

First of all, one begins with a paragraph which deals with a subject of vital concern to the people at the particular season of the year. In June, for example, one might use the passage about the Lord Jesus at the wedding.[4] Throughout this sermon, as in every other where he appears, the Lord Jesus should be at the center. In each of the Gospels, almost every preaching paragraph is about him. Hence the subject of this sermon may be, "The Glory of Our Lord's Personality."

After a few words of introduction, appropriate to the time and place, one points out the glory of our Lord's human interests. Now, as then, he is concerned about people, about the home, and about marriage. Next one calls attention to

---

[4] John 2:1-11; the text is verse 11.

96

the glory of his social sympathies. He cares when things go awry in the kitchen, when plans collapse, whenever joy is under a cloud. Nothing on earth is foreign to him. Best of all, one dwells upon the glory of his divine power. He transforms failure into success, and sorrow into joy. He can even transform a sinner into a saint. Such facts show that his glory is the outshining of the goodness which dwells only in God. Is it any wonder that his disciples believed on him? When they beheld his glory they saw in him the attractive goodness of God.

Second, one chooses a passage which relates concrete facts rather than abstract truth. One may find it easier to prepare sermons from the other Gospels than from John, which contains a good deal of high doctrine. In the Church today there is a crying need for the preaching of doctrine. But as a rule one can deal with a doctrine more readily in a textual or a topical sermon. For example, the new birth is a blessed mystery, a mystery of light, about which one ought to preach. But one should hesitate before attempting to expound the paragraph in which our Lord tells Nicodemus about the mystery of being born again.[5] In later years, however, after one has had experience in dealing with simple paragraphs, one can take up these high and holy words from John. The way to preach about them is to let the truth shine forth in the face of our blessed Lord.

Third, one chooses a paragraph which deals with a person in whom the hearer is interested. Apart from the Lord Jesus, the most interesting person in the Gospels is Peter. Down in the heart of the man in the pew is the feeling that he himself is

---

[5] John 3:1-13.

much like Peter. Hence the layman ought to enjoy hearing a sermon from the paragraph which tells how Andrew, an ordinary man, brings his more talented brother to Jesus.[6] Why not use this paragraph as the basis for a sermon, "Winning a Man for Christ"? Why not make these facts seem as dramatic as they really are? In the ideal preaching paragraph, the Lord Jesus appears with one or more persons much like those who sit in the rear pew.

Fourth, one singles out a paragraph which shows a few persons in action. In the Sermon on the Mount, for example, the easiest paragraph to make luminous is the one about the man who builds his house upon the rock.[7] The action here is dramatic. These words from the lips of our Lord have hands and feet. In the King James Bible this paragraph consists of 107 words. Every word would be clear to a boy ten years of age, the sort of boy who loves to build. In the Master's two sentences there is a balance even more beautiful than in the two parts of the first Psalm. In the former passage there are at least sixteen words or phrases which suggest action. Such a preacher sees what he says.

Read the paragraph aloud and listen for the scraping of the trowel on the stone. A little later, listen for the swish of the rising waters, and the rushing of the mighty wind. Last of all, listen for the crashing of the house that was built upon the sand. To the man who has put the savings of his lifetime into the building of the cottage which is to shelter him and his wife during their declining years, such a succession of sounds is almost as tragic as the trump of doom.

---

[6] John 1:35-42.
[7] Matt. 7:24-7.

98

In other words, the appeal here is to what Bunyan calls "eye-gate," as well as to "ear-gate." [8]   Likewise in preaching the sermon, one should get the man in the pew to see, to feel, to act.

HANDLING THE MATERIALS

Important as it is to select a suitable paragraph, much more important is it to handle the materials with skill and care. A helpful piece of pulpit interpretation may come out of a paragraph which does not conform to the foregoing specifications, which are chiefly for the man who is learning how to handle his homiletical tools.   If a man did not know how to preach, he might choose a paragraph which is pure gold, and yet bring out a sorry substitute for a sermon.   Like Aaron, the would-be biblical preacher might complain: "I cast it into the fire, and there came out this calf!" [9]   In other words, excellence in preaching is never a happy accident.   When one has found the right paragraph, the real work has only begun. How, then, should one handle the materials?

First, one masters the paragraph in its setting.   After one is familiar with the background, one should begin to look at the paragraph as a whole.   One should then take it apart, to examine each word or phrase with the skill of an exegete. This is where one makes use of the Greek or the Hebrew, with an exegetical commentary or two.   Thus one learns to examine inconspicuous details.   For example, in preaching from the parable about the talents,[10] one gives careful heed

---

[8] *The Holy War.*
[9] Exod. 32:24b; cf. the famous sermon by Phillips Brooks, "The Fire and the Calf," *Sermons,* Dutton, 1910, III, 43-64.
[10] Matt. 25:14-30.

to the principle on which the owner distributed the money to the different men. He gave to each "according to his several ability." Whereas in modern speech a talent means a certain sort of God-given ability—as for music—in the parable a talent evidently means an opportunity to be useful. A certain man has some special ability; God affords him an opportunity to use this ability helpfully. If he is faithful, God gives him the chance to use it twice as much. The reward for work well done is more work to do. But if a man is not faithful, God permits him to lose the opportunity for usefulness.

Second, one determines the exact purpose of the coming sermon. At the top of the working sheet one may write out the purpose, as a reminder that one is going into the pulpit with a message from the King for his servant in the pew. In preparing to preach about the parable of the talents, the purpose has to do with trusteeship. "Let me persuade my hearer to dedicate himself to a life of service, and to do so now." As soon as one gets the lay hearer to make this decision, in humble reliance on the grace of God, one finds no insuperable difficulty in persuading him to perform any other known duty. This sort of preaching is intensely practical. It aims to win a verdict for God, here and now. As G. Campbell Morgan often says, if the man in the pulpit is not moving the will to action, he is not preaching.

Third, in the light of this controlling purpose one takes from the paragraph as much material as one needs, and no more. In twenty-five minutes or less one cannot make every detail luminous, but one should be able to heighten what one selects for special emphasis. In preaching about the talents, for instance, one need not deal with all three of the men. Since only the occasional hearer is a man of genius— with five talents which he can double by faithful use—why not single out for special emphasis the man with two talents? The topic of the resulting sermon may be, "The Religion of the Average Man."

If one wishes something hard, one may throw the spotlight upon the man who hid his lone talent in the earth. But one must be careful lest one awaken sympathy for the man who failed to do his duty. At Princeton University Chapel, after an able sermon by a visiting professor from Yale, who dealt chiefly with the one-talent man, a sophomore said to another, "That poor fish got gypped!"

In less skillful hands, a paragraph sermon may be like the wrong sort of teaching in an adult Bible class. There is no selection, no omission, no heightening. Nothing is striking, or memorable, or even significant. Doubtless the man in the pulpit is striving to be a "good and faithful servant." In his zeal to be an expositor, however, he may forget that he is called to be a preacher. Preaching is the interpretation of religious facts in order to achieve a definite purpose. In preparing the sermon one should look each fact squarely in the face and ask it a question: "Can you help me reach my goal? If not, stand aside." If the resulting sermon is simple, the layman will be glad. If it is semi-expository, that may be exactly what the situation calls for. Preach!

Fourth, gradually arrange the materials in good homiletical form. In a teaching sermon good form is largely a matter of order. Often the best plan is to arrange the materials as they occur in the passage. For example, in preaching from the paragraph where our Lord tells about religion and life in terms of love,[11] the subject may be, "The Meaning of Religion as Love." After a brief problem approach in which one raises the question, "What is religion?" one turns to the Lord Jesus for the answer. It is threefold: religion means that a man should love God supremely, love his neighbor largely, and love himself last. What an arrangement! It has unity, and order, with the sort of climactic helpfulness which means that the man in the pew is looking upon himself as he is in the eyes of God. The arrangement comes directly out of the passage.

But what about originality? An occasional preacher will sacrifice almost anything in order to seem unique. Hence he almost invariably puts the big idea toward the end of the sermon. On the other hand, the present-day psychologist says that in public speaking as in preparing advertising copy one should put first what one wishes the other person to remember.[12] At intervals one should repeat the dominant idea. If it should come last, how could one repeat it often? For object lessons of such preaching—putting the large idea first, and repeating it often—study the sermons of Harry Emerson Fosdick.[13] Evidently he knows psychology as well as homiletics.

In the preaching class one day a young theologue even tried to improve the order of the Ten Commandments. In leading up to a hypothetical series, he proposed to say: "Firstly, we shall consider the Second Table, and secondly, we shall in-

---

[11] Matt. 22:34-40.

[12] *The Psychology of the Audience*, by H. L. Hollingsworth, American Book Co., 1935, pp. 86, 98, 100.

[13] E.g., the sermon, "Handling Life's Second-Bests," in *The Hope of the World*, Harper, 1933, pp. 69-77.

vestigate the First." If he had gone out into a village church with such a specimen of cross-eyed homiletics, a canny Scotch elder might have protested, "Mon, put the first thing first!"

CONVEYING THE MESSAGE

In preaching from the paragraph one usually gives the right of way to the positive. Thus one follows the example of the Master Preacher. When he wishes to make a sort of motion picture by using simple words, he puts first the man who builds upon the rock. Then he heightens the effect by picturing the one who builds upon the sand. Thus our Lord shows us how to preach as well as how to live. This same principle—stressing the positive—shines forth from the sermons of Robertson and Spurgeon, as well as Brooks and Clow. Each of them stressed the Master's "Thou shalt," rather than the scribes' "Thou shalt not." In fact, one of Robertson's maxims about preaching calls for "the establishment of positive truth, instead of the negative destruction of error." [14] Preach positively, not negatively!

Especially in the New Testament, the biblical emphasis is upon "The Everlasting Yea." Occasionally, however, our Lord puts the negative first. He puts first what he wishes us to remember most vividly. He does so in speaking about treasures on earth and treasures in heaven.[15] He wishes us to remember the folly of covetousness. In like manner, the preacher ought sometimes to throw the searchlight upon sin. But the man whose mind works philosophically rather than biblically is likely to overdo the business of stressing the evil

---

[14] *Life and Letters,* by S. A. Brooke, London, 1873-75, II, 153.
[15] Matt. 6:19-21.

rather than the good. One of the surest ways to correct the tendency towards stressing the secondary rather than the primary truth is to interpret each passage as it stands. Put the first thing first!

As a rule one follows the order of the ideas in the passage. But one should feel free to arrange the materials according to a pattern of one's own making. In all such matters one's own will is the master. As a wise builder one can secure most of the materials for the sermon out of a certain quarry. Then one should arrange the materials according to one's purpose. For example, in preaching from the most vital paragraph in the Sermon on the Mount,[16] one's plan would depend upon whether one desired to stress the Christian conception of the Kingdom, the Christian attitude toward money, or the Christian cure for worry.

This is one of the most fruitful preaching paragraphs in the First Gospel. Hence it is all the more necessary to select and arrange what one wishes to make luminous. Anyone who endeavored to present in one sermon all the truths of this paragraph, and in the original order, would be attempting the impossible. On the other hand, by turning to Alexander McLaren's sermon from this paragraph one can see how a master builder takes from the quarry only such stones as he needs for the new house, and then arranges them in a fashion all his own. The resulting expository sermon is most satisfying.[17]

McLaren's text, according to his custom, is brief. The essence of it is this: "Take no thought for your life." This

---

[16] Matt. 6:19-34.
[17] *Sermons Preached in Manchester*, first series, Macmillan, 1883, pp. 235-49.

injunction against worry rings out from the paragraph three times. The Master's three emphases suggest the three parts of the sermon. The subject is "Anxious Care." The line of thought is simple. The introductory paragraph calls attention to the distinction between anxious care and laudable foresight. The sermon proper grows out of three basic propositions:

> Nature shows that anxious care is needless.
> Revelation shows that anxious care is heathenish.
> Providence shows that anxious care is futile.

Any minister who reads the sermon will wonder why he never saw these three truths shining out from the paragraph. If he attempts to preach from it, with the emphasis upon the Christian cure for worry, he will find it hard to depart from McLaren's line of thought. Instead of trying to improve on his basic pattern, or else ignore it, why not simply borrow, and then give credit? The people will know that McLaren got these ideas from the Master. They will thank God for the new light which streams on the old problem of living without worry. They will thank him, too, for a minister who is like McLaren in having a keen sense of homiletical divination.

A careful study of McLaren's sermons will show that a teaching message should have sturdy structure. The structure should stand out. As in a working horse, there should be a strong bony framework. However, the passerby should see the horse on the bones, not the bones in the horse. The reason for stressing structure in a biblical sermon—more than in other sorts of preaching, such as the "inspirational"—is that the popular biblical interpreter is a teacher. In teaching from the Bible what matters is that the hearer shall learn the truth of God, and then live in its holy light. He should understand. He should remember. He should go forth resolved to begin doing God's holy will.

From this point of view, which is practical, why spend twenty-five minutes in talking about a parable, if at the end of the sermon an impressionable young hearer is simply to feel that some person long ago was "gypped"? This sort of biblical preaching is almost as ineffectual as the famous battle of Blenheim:

> " 'But what good came of it at last?'
> Quoth little Peterkin,
> 'Why, that I cannot tell,' said he,
> 'But 'twas a famous victory.' "

In other words, one should think more about what concerns the hearer than about what the passage means. While the warp of the message should come out of the chosen paragraph, the woof should come out of human life and thought today. If the occasional semi-secular preacher errs in relying too largely on present-day materials, the biblical interpreter is tempted to use such facts too sparingly. Opinions differ about the wisdom of making frequent allusions to literature, art, and science. Perhaps the occasional preacher spends too much of his spare time in those secular fields. But the average biblical preacher would be more interesting and more helpful if he tempered his message with more sweetness and light from those other sources. The rule is, as in playing a game, do whatever is sure to advance the ball.

BEING SIMPLE

The preceding discussion may have made the paragraph

sermon seem complicated. But it should not be so. In addressing all sorts of people, some of whom are uncultured, the minister should make every message simple and attractive. In the spring, for example, everyone in the rural parish is thinking about sowing seeds in garden and field, just as everyone in the city is longing to get out into the open and watch the growth of seeds that he has planted. Hence the minister preaches about what is mistakenly called "the parable of the sower." [18] The emphasis is not upon the sower, or the seed, but upon the state of the soil.

The topic may be "A Parable for the Farmer," or else "A Parable from the Garden." The theme, or key sentence, may be this: "The effectiveness of the sermon depends largely on the state of the hearer's soul." Even if the sower is the Lord Jesus, and if the seed is from the Bible, the effect will be lasting and blessed only if the hearer is ready to receive the truth. In all four stages of the parable the same sower is handling the same sort of seed in the same skillful manner. At the harvest time the varying results are due to the diverse conditions of the soil. Chemically, there is no difference. That lies in what one may call the degrees of "preparedness." Even the city lad knows that poor soil skillfully prepared will produce a more bountiful crop than rich soil not properly prepared.

The parable suggests four lines of thought. Each calls for a simple declarative sentence. The careful expositor seldom uses a phrase where he can employ a sentence. The sentence is more complete and more specific. Hence it has greater teaching value. In preaching about this parable each

---

[18] Matt. 13:1-9, 18-23. In reading the lesson one may omit verses 10-17.

main sentence translates figure into fact. The ensuing discussion has to do with the fact in the light of the figure. In order to talk intelligently in terms of soil, one needs to know a good deal about such matters here at home, as well as in the Holy Land.[19] If one gets mixed up in one's allusions to farm and garden, it may be hard for the hearer to feel sure that one knows much about heaven.

This is the first main sentence: "The wayside soil represents the indifferent hearer." The figure refers to the beaten pathway, which countless passing feet have trodden down so that seeds strewn on the solid surface lie there until the sparrows swoop down and snatch them away. The picture is that of the man who is present at public worship only in his body. His mind is at his office, or else out on the golf links. In a sense he hears, but he does not understand. If the preacher is doing his part well, the reason the layman does not understand is that he does not care. His soul evidently needs the plowshare and the harrow. Under present-day conditions, however, the indifferent man is likely not to be present in church.

Second, "The rocky soil represents the superficial hearer." This figure, too, is unique. It refers to the thin layer of soil which covers the ledge of impenetrable rock. In a county of southern Kansas there is a surface coating of fertile soil, beneath which is "hardpan." In such surface soil the seeds spring up more quickly than they would if the substratum did not hold the rain and the heat. But later in the season, when there is little rain and much heat, the tender shoots shrivel and

---

[19] See *The Historical Geography of the Holy Land,* by George Adam Smith, London, 1931.

die. The picture is that of the person whom almost every sermon moves to tears, but whom nothing ever impels to bring forth fruit. Such an impractical hearer may need a tremendous, crashing, shattering explosion in the soul. In planting a tree where there is hardpan, the Kansas farmer digs a hole and uses dynamite to break up the solid substratum. Then he plants his tree. In five or six years he begins to gather his fruit.

Third, "The thorny soil represents the worldly hearer." The figure is clear. The soil is rich. Since it raises a profuse thicket of thorns, it could produce a bountiful crop of wheat. But the soil has not strength enough to produce both thorns and wheat. Hence the wheat languishes and dies. Wheat requires soil that is cultivated; thorns grow wild. That is why the thrifty Dutch farmer detests soil that is "dirty." Out of thorns which a careful farmer would not have suffered to survive, cruel men once platted the crown which they put on the head of our Redeemer. Is it pushing the facts too far to say that man's worldliness crucified the King of Kings?

This third part of the tale points to the man who is trying to make the utmost possible out of both worlds. Hence he loses one world without gaining the other. According to the parable, worldliness [20] is only another name for worry about things, and for love of money. How can the truth of God have its way in the heart of the housemother who is busy and troubled about many things, or in the mind of the business-man who has sold his soul to the devil? For an object lesson of mercenary worldliness, see the main character in a current

---

[20] See F. W. Robertson, "Worldliness," in *Sermons*, London, 1889, II, 145-59.

novel, *The Citadel.*[21] In a fashionable part of West London a brilliant Welsh physician sells his soul for gold. Before it is too late, he comes to himself, and fights his way back to his early ideals. Unfortunately, however, his way back is not that of the Bible.

Fourth, "The good soil represents the ideal hearer." This soil is the same, chemically, as that which we have been thinking about, but in the last part of the tale the soil is properly prepared. The emphasis is upon the hearer's attitude toward the truth of God. In the three versions of the parable, each of the Synoptic Gospels speaks about the ideal hearer in a different way. Matthew says that he understands the Word; this is the point of view of the teacher. Mark says that the ideal hearer accepts the truth; this is the point of view of the practical man. Luke says that the ideal hearer holds fast that which is good; this is the point of view of the man who thinks first about personality. In any case, the ideal hearer is the one for whom the pastor daily renders thanks to God.

The final test of the soil comes at the harvest. What farmer in Iowa would not rejoice if by sowing a bushel and a peck of wheat to the acre he could be certain to harvest thirty-seven and a half bushels? That would be thirtyfold. But God is waiting and eager to give sixty or even a hundredfold. He is that sort of God!

What a paragraph for a message at the time of the year when the winter has fled! But keep the sermon simple, and be sure to make it shine.

----

[21] By A. J. Cronin, Little, Brown, 1937.

CHAPTER VI

THE PARAGRAPH COURSE

As a young minister I find that I am losing a great deal of time owing to my methods of study. Since I need a definite plan I have decided to undertake a study of the Fourth Gospel. I should like to preach from it connectedly, but I should not anounce my plan to the people. Have you any suggestions?" This request comes from a young pastor in Mississippi. His letter shows that he is already on his way out of the woods. Still he should welcome a little advice and encouragement from one who has been over the road.

This is part of the reply: "While you are learning how to do this difficult sort of pulpit work, why not begin with Mark rather than John? Although many of us believe that the latter book is the greatest in the Bible, we all find the other one easier to handle. Whichever book you select, there is no reason why the passages need be long or consecutive. It would require a good deal of ability to deal with large sections of either Gospel, and a vast deal of time to take up either of them by paragraphs. Some passages, such as the thirteenth chapter of Mark, would cause acute difficulty. So why not master the book as a whole, and then prepare a course of sermons from selected paragraphs?"

PREACHING FROM MARK

The plan calls for a succession of sermons. In order

to be specific let us think of the Sunday mornings between Christmas and Easter. If during the period leading up to Christmas one has been preaching from the Old Testament, thus showing how God reveals himself in the experience of men like ourselves, the obvious time to begin preaching from Mark is on the Sunday after Christmas. (If one were preaching from Luke or Matthew, which deal with the birth of Christ, one would begin about the middle of December.) A week before the new course starts, the bulletin may carry the following announcement: "It will help the minister in his preaching if the members of the congregation will read the Gospel of Mark at family prayers and in private devotions. Between now and Easter every morning sermon will be from this Gospel."

In the opening sermon one may present the book as a whole, perhaps under the heading, "The Gospel in Motion Pictures." Without anticipating what is to come in later sermons, one tries first of all to make the book seem so attractive that everyone present will determine to read it through the same afternoon. Some of the people will read the book again and again. When they have a definite book to read, and a practical reason for doing so, they will find in the Scriptures new interest and unexpected helpfulness. They will likewise have a new incentive for coming to church regularly. They will begin to feel that preaching is a co-operative enterprise. Every winter they will wish their minister to follow the same plan. Thus he can make the round of the Gospels once every four years. The plan has untold possibilities.

In the course every sermon should center in Christ. It would be easy to preach from Mark twelve or fifteen times without once bringing the hearer face to face with Christ. The first sermon might be about John Mark; it might even be a mere skeleton of his book. Succeeding messages might be about John the Baptist, the paralytic, the man with the withered hand, with a succession of other interesting men and women. After a while the course might call for sermons about Judas, Pilate, and Barabbas. But where is the Lord Jesus? Is there no room for preaching directly about him in the Church which he died to redeem? Since this Gospel, like each of the others, was written to tell about Christ, every sermon in the course should be primarily about him. Whenever he is in the picture, he should be at the center, with the light full in his face. If he is not to be in the picture, why paint it?

This is largely what our most spiritual laymen mean by asking for Gospel sermons. Strange to tell, it is not easy to preach about Christ week after week without losing one's touch with the realities of today. But such preaching is still possible. After one of our students had visited a well-known church in Northern Jersey a number of Sundays in succession, he reported to his professor of homiletics: "That young minister preaches more about Jesus than anyone else whom I have ever heard." The report gladdened the heart of the teacher, especially since he knew that week after week through the winter the young man's sermons would come closer to the Cross. It is no accident that in Mark, as in the other Gospels, there are various foreshadowings of the Cross, and that the latter part of the Second Gospel is full of its blessed light.[1] True Christian preaching always centers in Christ.

---

[1] See *History and the Gospel*, by C. H. Dodd, Scribner, 1938, p. 72.

PREACHING FROM THE BIBLE

If possible, it is wise to study about three months in advance. Allowing one hour a day and five days in the week for advance study, the pastor will find the three-months period all too brief. The plan of study is simple.

First, one masters the book as a whole. One reads it straight through, preferably at a single sitting. One reads it through again, and even the third time, to get a clear vision of what it reveals concerning the earthly life of our Lord. Then one analyzes the book by paragraphs. One finds out what each paragraphs means, and what bearing it has on the message of the book as a whole. Of course one writes down the preaching lesson of each paragraph, with anything else of interest and value. By preserving in one's files the results of these analytical studies, one gradually accumulates an inexhaustible store of preaching materials.

Second, one chooses paragraphs with preaching messages sure to prove interesting and helpful to the people in the parish. The number of sermons will depend on the number of Sundays between Christmas and Easter. If on any Lord's Day something arises to interrupt the course, no harm will ensue. At this season, fortunately, no special days call for semi-secular sermons. As for February with its birthdays of national heroes, such occasions suggest timely illustrations. In preaching about the kindness of Jesus, for instance, one can use specific facts about Lincoln or Lee, each of whom excelled in this quiet grace. But no national hero ought for a single sermon to usurp the place of Jesus Christ. He alone can redeem the soul, bless the home, or rule over the world. Especially during the harvest season of the year, between

Christmas and Easter, every morning sermon ought to be primarily about Christ.

The arrangement of the sermon topics should occasion no difficulty. One simply follows the order of the passages as they appear in Mark. The idea is to keep the people looking forward, and to keep them turning the pages of the book ever in the same direction. For instance, when they come to church the second Sunday morning in February they need not know where in Mark the minister will find his text. But they should be keenly aware that every Lord's Day is drawing them closer to the Cross. So inviting are these successive scenes in the earthly life of our Lord that one desires to preach from a part of every chapter. But it is better to pass by a chapter here or there, so as to leave enough time for sermons about the trial and the death of our Lord.[2] That is where the sinner is likely to find the Saviour, and where the saint is sure to find peace.

Third, one gradually accumulates and arranges the materials for the various sermons. In addition to what one finds in the chosen paragraphs, one assembles the results of reading and pastoral experience, as well as the fruits of hours spent in meditation and prayer. Anyone who tries this method of mastering a book as a whole and in its parts, with special study of chosen paragraphs, will be amazed at the amount and the variety of the materials which keep coming to his hands. Before Christmas Day he should have in store ready for use practically all the materials he will need for twelve or fifteen successive sermons from Mark. However, he should let each message come to its final form only a few days before

---

[2] See *The Trial and Death of Jesus Christ*, by James Stalker, Doran, 1894.

delivery. Otherwise the message might seem stale. However forehanded, the minister should never serve food which has lain in cold storage and has to be warmed over.

For object lessons showing how these principles work, look at the list below. The topics appear in the bulletin and elsewhere only one at a time. The texts appear not at all. But in each sermon there is much emphasis upon the text. For example, in the message about the Lord Jesus as the Ideal Physician, there is much about his sympathy. It sounds forth in the text: "I will; be thou clean." In the sermon about the Christian use of Sunday, the stress is upon three sayings of our Lord, with a slight verbal change in the last one: "The Sabbath was made for man," "The Son of Man is Lord of the Sabbath Day," and "It is lawful to do good on the Sabbath Day." In the list below, the topic for the opening sermon is not the same as the one suggested above, "The Gospel in Motion Pictures." Whatever the topic, it should dominate the sermon.

The Gospel of Christian Service .... Mark 1:1
The Healer of Body and Soul .... Mark 1:40-45
The Christian Use of Sunday .... Mark 2:23-3:5
The Christian Conquest of Fear .... Mark 4:35-41
The Christian Cure for Race Prejudice .... Mark 7:24-30
The Practical Sympathy of Jesus .... Mark 8:1-9
The Wonder of Our Lord's Personality ..... Mark 9: 1-10
The Christian Idea of Service .... Mark 10:35-45
The Lordship of Jesus in Our City .... Mark 11:1-11
The Practical Meaning of Our Religion .... Mark 12:28-31
The Christian Uses of Money .... Mark 14:3-11
The Sin of Being Ashamed .... Mark 14:66-72
The Barabbas Theory of the Atonement .. Mark 15:1-15
The Crucifixion of Our King .... Mark 15:22-32

APPEALING TO THE LAYMAN

Let us glance over one of these sermons, the one about "The Christian Conquest of Fear." Fear is the strongest emotion of the human heart; that is, the strongest except love. "Perfect love casteth out fear." [3] Fear causes war and panic, suicide and every other sort of diabolical disorder. In the typical parish today, many of the people are like the disciples in the boat on Galilee. Timorous souls today ought to hear the Master saying through his servant in the pulpit: "Why are ye so fearful? How is it that ye have no faith?" [4] Thus the sermon has to do with the contrast between fear and faith; that is, between the human and the divine.

The cause of fear is lack of faith in God. The cure of fear is faith in the Living Christ. Here, then, is a typical Robertsonian text. It calls for two key sentences, each of which should be about the Living Christ. First, he is ever with us amid the storms of life. Second, he is waiting to quiet our human fears. He knows. He cares. He is tender to sympathize and mighty to save. He is able to do exceeding abundantly above all that we ask or think. Even if the storm is not raging in any man's soul, or out in his little world, the time to prepare for the storm is now.

During the minor depression in 1907 a well-known bank in an Ohio city was about to go on the rocks. If the bank had failed widows and orphans and benevolent institutions would have lost their all. They had intrusted their savings

[3] I John 4:18b.
[4] Mark 4:40.

to the bank because of their confidence in the president, who for years had been an elder in his church. As he strove in vain to steer the bank away from the rocks, he became so wrought up nervously that he could not eat or sleep. In a sense he was not worth his salt. One night, after tossing from pillow to pillow, he rose and looked round for something to read. Not seeing anything else of interest, he picked up his Bible, and for the first time in his life he read one of the major books straight through without a stop.

The book that he read was Mark. He must have been guided by the Spirit, for Mark is a book of action. Hence it appealed to the businessman. As he read paragraph after paragraph, he forgot about himself and his bank. At the end of the reading, which took only an hour and a quarter, he closed his eyes and said with a sigh of relief: "O Lord Jesus, I thank thee that thou art living now, and that thou art here." Then he lay down and slept. The next morning, after his loved ones had awakened him, he ate a hearty breakfast and then walked down to the bank. He found it in as critical a state as it had been the day before. But the president was a new man. He had faith and courage. He determined by God's grace to keep that bank open, honorably. So he did. Our religion still works!

If the bank had failed, because the president had lost his grip on God and on himself, his church would have cared for some of the widows and orphans whom his lack of faith had made destitute. Then people would have looked at that relief work and exclaimed: "What a demonstration of practical Christianity!" But through reading this Gospel of Christian Service the banker discovered that the biblical way to relieve poverty is to prevent it. Instead of arranging to have a splendidly equipped ambulance waiting at the foot of the precipice, he thought it more Christlike to build a sturdy fence at the top. Is there no call for this brand of religion today? Where can the business man find it more surely than by reading the Gospel of Mark?

Between Palm Sunday and Easter this sort of layman welcomes a series of special sermons. These too may be from Mark. Ordinarily the special meetings come at night. But in a downtown church the best time may be the noon hour. In either case there is no meeting on Saturday. During Holy Week in downtown Pittsburgh Clarence E. Macartney one year recently spoke at noon about "The Truce of God." [5] Here is what he wrote for the last page of the attractive folder which announced the series:

These sermons are all based on incidents of the last day of our Lord upon earth. In every sermon we shall see Christ face to face with souls. To each of them he gave a word, a look, a warning, which for a moment flashed before him the opportunity to choose Christ and eternal life. This moment came like a Truce of God, when he grants the soul a brief reprieve. These special sermons before Easter, centering about the Passion and Death of Christ, come like a Truce of God. Thousands of souls need that Truce. Pray earnestly that while the Truce lasts, they shall choose eternal life.

PREACHING FROM ACTS

After Easter the logical plan would call for preaching about the Lord's post-Resurrection appearances and interviews, one at a time. Perhaps that will be the program a year hence.

---

[5] This title shows that the preacher is a lover of history. For the term "Truce of God" see *The Encyclopedia Britannica*.

But in training the people to read the Bible by books, there is a distinct advantage in turning to Acts soon after Easter. This plan calls for three months of preparatory spade work in the study. During the long weeks before Easter, while one is preaching from Mark or Luke, one can devote at least an hour a day to the Book of Acts. In these hours of study, as in the resulting sermons, one should keep one's gaze fixed upon the Living Christ, not on Peter and Paul, except as Christ makes himself known through these apostles. Because of Christ's indwelling, through the Holy Spirit the leaders of the Early Christian Church "out-lived the pagan, out-thought him, and out-died him." [6] Herein lies the secret of Christian radiance. For living examples, look at the following subjects:

The Power of God in the Lives of Men . . . . Acts 1:6-8
The Revival in the Church Today . . . . Acts 2:1-4
The Christian Secret of Power . . . . Acts 3:1-10
The Practical Business of the Church . . . . Acts 6:1-6
The Winning of a Strong Man to Christ . . . . . . Acts 8:26-40
The Beginning of a Mighty Man's Faith . . . . Acts 9:1-9
The Appeal of Christ to a Leader of Men . . . . . Acts 10:34-43
The Conversion of a Business Woman . . . . Acts 16:13-15
The Reality of Adult Conversion . . . . Acts 16:25-33
The Worship of the Unknown God . . . . Acts 17:22-34
The Glory of the Clean Conscience . . . . Acts 24:10-31
The Eloquence of Christian Experience . . . . . . Acts 26:24-29
The Christian Secret of Leadership . . . . Acts 27:21-26

Let us glance at two of these sermons. One is about "The Reality of Adult Conversion." In a certain parish some of the good women had acquired their theological notions chiefly from itinerant evangelists of the lurid sort. More than one of

---

[6] *The Jesus of History*, by T. R. Glover, Doran, 1917, p. 200.

those women feared that she never had been born again, because she could not tell the day and the hour of her second birth. If the incoming pastor had attacked the problem openly, as he was tempted to do, he might have caused heartburnings. No normal woman wishes to have her minister speak in public about the maladies of her soul. Fortunately the pastor waited until the course of sermons from Acts led to the sixteenth chapter. Without resorting to the technical terms of psychology and theology, he pointed to Lydia, the business woman, as an object lesson of "quiet and comfortable conversion," and to the Philippian jailer as an example of "sudden and violent conversion." [7] This message from God's Holy Book seems to have dispelled the mist and the fog from more than one timorous soul.

Another message is about "The Christian Secret of Leadership." This sermon would be especially fitting at a time of crisis in the Mediterranean world, or anywhere else at sea. After one has read to the people the twenty-seventh chapter—it may be in two sections—one need do nothing more to arouse interest. The chapter is the world's classic account of a storm at sea. That is a subject which appeals to every heart. In Luke's narrative, however, the climactic emphasis is not upon the storm but upon the Living Christ. He makes his will known to his servant: "Fear not, Paul . . . . God hath given thee all them that sail with thee." [8] Herein lies the secret of leadership.

Evidently Paul has been spending long days and nights in prayer. He has been praying, not for himself but for the

---

[7] See W. Mackintosh Mackay, *The Disease and Remedy of Sin*, Doran, 1919, pp. 142-74.
[8] Acts 27:24.

others who are in peril. When the time comes for him to act, he is ready. In the name of the Lord Jesus, in whom no one else on board believes, this prisoner who has never been a seaman takes command of the ship. Thus he is the Lord's agent in preserving the lives of 276 men. Would that every congregation with that many members had a man like Paul to lead in the hour of crisis!

Fifty years ago when T. DeWitt Talmage was probably the most popular pulpiteer in America he delivered an evening sermon from this chapter. His emphasis was upon the closing verse, which he used somewhat allegorically: "And the rest, some on boards, and some on broken pieces of the ship. And so it came to pass that they escaped all safe to land." [9] His message struck home to the hearts of a bride and groom who were enjoying their honeymoon in our capital city. Years later an aged grandmother in Ohio used to tell her pastor how she and her young husband, spellbound, had listened to that sermon, and how through all the vicissitudes of the passing years they had lived in the light of the vision which thus came to them from God. Although they knew but little about the sea, they learned to think of their lives together in terms of Acts twenty-seven, and of their final homegoing as landing safely on the other shore, after a voyage marked by many storms.

Any such sermon, however dramatic and thrilling, is doubly effective as an integral part of a course or a series. This is the testimony of the late Burnett H. Streeter, who was for years one of the brightest luminaries at Oxford University:

---

[9] Acts 27:44.

The pulpit is a far less effective instrument than it might be for the edification of the pew. This is largely due to the haphazard and unsystematic way in which the subject of the sermon is usually selected. Every pastor should have a definite and well thought-out scheme, at least for some weeks in advance, if not for the whole year, of course reserving to himself the liberty to depart from it for good reasons. . . . .

A connected series on any subject by a man of moderate ability will make far more permanent impression than an equal number of isolated sermons by a brilliant preacher. The congregation recall what was said the last time; they look forward to what will be said next time. . . . . The uncharitable can no longer surmise that the subject of the exhortation is determined by the text that happened to come into his head on Saturday morning while shaving. And a congregation which feels that it is being taken seriously will take the preacher seriously; it will attend to what he has to say; and attention is the primary condition of really taking in a lesson. . . . . No man can give the best he has to give in a single sermon. In a course of sermons he has some chance of making a definite and permanent impression.[10]

The Oxford divine is thinking about conditions in England, where the parish minister normally has only a single charge. But fortunately this sort of consecutive preaching is possible when one has several preaching stations. In fact, by some such plan, modified to meet local conditions, one should be able to work more effectively than by hit-and-miss ways of preaching. For example, if one enters the circuit in September, one may rely at first upon biographical sermons from the Old Testament. Thus the emphasis every Sunday is upon man's need of God. As one draws near to Christmas one may plan something more constructive, as well as more intensive, but

---

[10] *Concerning Prayer*, by B. H. Streeter et al., Macmillan, 1916, pp. 275-77. Used by permission of The Macmillan Company.

still quite simple. In other words, one may begin preaching from the Gospel of Luke.

To be specific, let us think about Cream Ridge, a rural chapel where one holds services every Sunday at three o'clock. On the second or third Sunday in December the sermon is about "The Gospel of God's Grace"—a popular introduction to Luke—with special emphasis on our Lord as a lover of human beings one by one. On this day the most important announcement is that on the following Sunday, and at every succeeding service until Easter, the minister will preach from Luke, and that it will help him to do so if every member and friend of the congregation will read and pray over the Gospel of Luke. In many a parish where the people have been accustomed to heterogeneous preaching this pulpit notice would cause a pleasant stir.

Better still, the plan should prove helpful to the people's souls. It should give them a new incentive to read the Bible with open hearts and minds. Deprived as they are of a pastor's life and influence throughout the week, and often tempted to feel that the minister forgets all about them between Sundays, they should learn to look upon him as their guide into the meaning and the power of the Book. Accustomed as they are to planning the rotation of crops, and to the shifting of sheep from meadow to fold, they should look with respect upon the minister who has a plan for feeding his flock out of the Book.

As for the minister, he should profit even more. Distracted as he often is by the demands of various charges remote from each other and from his home, he should have a strong incentive to study his Bible every morning. If he becomes enthusiastic about learning to know his Bible, a book at a time, and if he learns how to use it as the basis of his preaching from week to week, he will find new joy and new profit in his morning hours of study. Since he has to prepare only one new message every week, he has all the greater opportunity to feed each of his flocks with the choicest food.

The heart of the whole matter is that practically every parish today is in need of a teaching ministry, and that the basis of the teaching ministry is the Bible, as it centers in Christ. Especially in preaching from one of the Gospels, the easiest way is to stress the paragraph.

CHAPTER VII

THE EXPOSITORY LECTURE

In a course of expository lectures one takes up in turn the various parts of the chosen book. As the basis of each sermon one uses a paragraph, or a cluster of related paragraphs; it may be an entire chapter. In theory the paragraph is more nearly ideal, but in practice the chapter is more often the unit. Whatever the size of the successive portions, one preaches straight through the book without omitting any part. This too is the theory. In practice the wise expository lecturer passes by any stone which he cannot lift and carry.

For object lessons of expository lectures, once used in the pulpit so effectively that they found their way into print and helped to make the preacher famous, turn to Alexander McLaren on the Psalms, or to George Adam Smith on Isaiah. The latter also writes about the Minor Prophets, but not on the same high level as in his treatment of Isaiah.[1] Even in the hands of such a master, success in popular lecturing depends partly on the selection of the book.

CHARTING THE COURSE

As a rule one begins with a book that is comparatively short. It ought preferably to be practical rather than doctrinal. For instance, take the Epistle of James. It presents few difficulties of interpretation. The subject is interesting, because it con-

---

[1] Each of these series is in *The Expositor's Bible.*

cerns the everyday living of the average man. While social problems emerge more than once, the discussion of them is from the point of view of the individual Christian. Since the Epistle of James is intensely practical it lends itself admirably to use after Easter. The purpose in preaching from the book is to guide the new convert, as well as the church member of longer standing, in doing the will of God seven days in the week.

The next thing is to master the book. One turns often to the commentary by Mayor,[2] but one depends much more upon reading the Epistle itself. One reads it straight through, several times. Thus one gradually formulates the subject, at least tentatively. It may be "The Meaning of a Man's Religion."[3] Then one analyzes the book by paragraphs. In the notes about each paragraph one puts down the tentative subject, the heart of the preaching message, and anything else of permanent interest or value. Much of this material will not find its way into the course, but will go into one's files for use in coming days. After a man has been in the ministry eight or ten years his files should contain the results of his studies in almost every book of the Bible.

On the basis of these notes about paragraphs one gradually plots the course. In James one can find a sermon in almost every paragraph. If one did that, the course might seem interminable. Since one is to announce the course only in general, and the specific subjects only from week to week, one need not keep the numbers down to four or five. If the

---

[2] *The Epistle of St. James,* by Joseph B. Mayor, Macmillan, 1913. See also *Practical and Social Aspects of Christianity,* by A. T. Robertson, Doran, 1915. While not a commentary, this work is suggestive.

[3] The key verse is Jas. 1:27.

interest of the people grows from week to week, naturally one may keep on preaching from James. But if their interest is likely to lag, one may cut across to another pasture. In any case it would scarcely be wise to continue preaching from James more than two or three months. The book is not so vital as others.

How, then, can one shorten the course? The easy way would be to pass by a paragraph now and again. For instance, there are three separate paragraphs about the rich man.[4] It may be embarrassing for the minister to broach the subject, especially if there is in the parish only one man of means, and if he is a problem. But in preaching through the book silence about money would be a mistake. One of the chief merits in expository lecturing is that it requires one to preach about delicate subjects that one might otherwise dodge. When the laymen know that the minister is preaching through a certain book, they expect him to interpret the book as it stands. Of course they in turn should receive every message as from the Lord. Nevertheless, there is no way of preaching biblical ethics painlessly.

Perhaps the best way to shorten the course without omitting anything vital is to combine related paragraphs. Why preach three sermons about the rich man, or two about temptation?[5] If the paragraphs on any subject are not consecutive, the reason is that the book is like a fugue melody, with recurrent emphasis on a few dominant notes. Without calling special attention to what one is doing, and still without concealment, one can put into a single sermon the substance of two or three related

---

[4] Jas. 1:9-11; 2:1-13; 5:1-6.
[5] Jas. 1:2-4; 1:12-15.

paragraphs, or make any other combination that one desires. What matters is that one should discuss frankly and clearly every practical problem to which the apostle devotes a paragraph or two. In a course of expository lectures, as in the Epistle of James, there may be some overlapping, but there should be little overlooking.

PREACHING FROM JAMES

Let us think about the introductory sermon. Since no person has ever succeeded in making a memorable outline of the book, one may present it topically. The subject of the opening sermon may be, "The Practical Meaning of Religion." [6] Pure religion is applied. The man who tries to keep his religion pure, as mathematics is pure, is sure to fail. Religion is as practical for a man's soul as water for his body. If water is already pure, the way to keep it so is to let it run. If it is not pure, running may help to cleanse it, but something more drastic may be required. In any case stagnant religion, so called, would be worse than none. The way for a man to preserve "the white flower of a blameless life," therefore, is to keep doing the will of God as revealed in the Book. There is no easy road to heaven's gate.

Such practical teachings are not in accord with certain kinds of present-day theology. The idea of showing one's religion by doing gentle deeds of mercy to the widow and the orphan sounds like what some of our European critics stigmatize as "crass American activism." That seems to mean depending upon the works of man, not the grace of God. Of course a person can go too far in either direction. On the right hand is

---

[6] The text is Jas. 1:27.

the rousing appeal for social action. In one of the best modern hymns of its kind this is the second stanza:

> "Rise up, ye men of God!
> His Kingdom tarries long;
> Bring in the day of brotherhood,
> And end the night of wrong." [7]

After one has joined in a song of Christian optimism one feels uplifted. But on sober second thought one asks how we sinful mortals can shorten the night of wrong, and thus bring in the day of brotherhood. When the Bible says something of the sort, literalistic critics make sport.[8] Perhaps they forget that this verse in the Bible, like the hymn, is poetic. There appears to be a need for such appeals to social action. But we ought to remember that the coming of the Kingdom depends upon God, and that he is waiting to use us as his humble servants.

On the other hand, as a reaction against our practical teachings about religion and life, a few of our friends go to the other extreme. In fact, a certain wag suggests that they ought to sing:

> "Sit down, O men of God!
> You cannot do a thing!
> When it is pleasing to God's will
> His Kingdom he will bring."

Speaking seriously, men of both schools agree that any spirit of passivity is foreign to James. In fact, there seems to be a tendency to preach from the Bible according to the elective system, which enables a man to dodge what he does not like.

---

[7] By William P. Merrill, 1911.
[8] See Josh. 10:12, 13.

Of course one could defend oneself for ignoring James by echoing what Martin Luther wrote about it as "an epistle of straw." But Luther was wise enough to know that straw has its uses. When he wrote these words he was merely comparing James with other books in the Bible, such as Romans. Elsewhere Luther refers to James as "a good book." Of course it is not so mighty as Romans or Hebrews, but in our part of the world we are fortunately free to preach from any book in the Bible, just as it stands.

However, one need not rush out to the rescue of James, or any other book in the Sacred Canon. The Bible is abundantly able to take care of itself. Indeed, it is waiting to fight our battles. Hence the wise interpreter refrains from controversy. The custom of the popular expositor is to explain his passage, proclaim his truth, and restrain his temper. Likewise does he keep silent concerning the vagaries of people who are not present. Whenever the interpreter preaches from the Holy Book, he should do nothing but preach.

For the initial sermon one may have a bird's-eye view of James. In it one discovers at least five clear lines of thought. Instead of going into any one of these fully, however, and thus anticipating what is to come in later sermons, one should simply state the five problems in terms of today, and then encourage the reader to seek the various solutions by reading the Epistle itself. If one were planning a short series, one might use these five problems as the rallying points for the evening sermons during a month with five Sundays. But in a longer course, in which one is "lecturing," the introductory message may well be a book sermon, with five headings. In each of them the organizing principle is that of contrast.

Pure religion in temptation and in trial
Pure religion in theory and in practice
Pure religion for the heart and for the tongue
Pure religion for the rich and for the poor
Pure religion for this world and for the next

Let us also think about the course as a whole. In the following list of subjects, the one for the opening sermon is different from the one which we have been considering. As with the introduction to a sermon, there are various good ways of leading up to a connected course. The nature of the introductory message depends upon one's purpose. The idea is to strike the dominant note of the entire course. In the opening sermon listed below, the emphasis would be upon James, the brother of our Lord, and upon the practical quality of his piety. Both in substance and in style, his little book is much like certain parts of the Old Testament, as well as the Sermon on the Mount. The same practical emphasis appears in the topics listed below. The course as thus outlined is unduly long. Otherwise it seems to require no comment.

The Apostle of Applied Christianity .... Jas. 1:1
The Joys of Enduring Temptation .... Jas. 1:2-4
The Cause of Unanswered Prayer .... Jas. 1:5-8
The Fading Joys of the Rich Man .... Jas. 1:9-11
The Practical Workings of Temptation .... Jas. 1:12-15
The Practical Meaning of Religion .... Jas. 1:19-27
The Sin of Snobbishness in Church .... Jas. 2:1-13
The Practical Meaning of Faith .... Jas. 2:14-26
The Perils of the Tongue .... Jas. 3:1-12
The Secret of Harmony among Men .... Jas. 3:13-18
The Cause of Strife among Men .... Jas. 4:1-10
The Folly of the Fault Finder .... Jas. 4:11, 12
The Folly of Counting on Tomorrow .... Jas 4:13-17
The Woes of the Idle Rich .... Jas. 5:1-6

PLANNING OTHER COURSES

After one has learned how to prepare a simple course of popular "lectures," and has led the people to like this sort of substantial fare, one may plan a course from a larger and more difficult book. It may be First Corinthians, which lends itself admirably to such uses. In preaching from a long book the obvious way to keep the number of sermons within bounds and still cover the field is to proceed by chapters. Ordinarily each chapter calls for a separate discourse, but here and there one may combine two or three chapters which are closely related.

In Second Corinthians, for example, one might use chapters eight and nine as the starting point for a sermon about giving money to Christ through the local church.[9] In these two chapters the apostle sets forth the basic principles about contributing to missions and current expenses. In preaching about trusteeship—a sort of preaching as difficult as it is vital— George W. Truett of the First Baptist Church in Dallas, Texas, seems to excel.[10] His example shows one how to present any such Christian duty by basing one's teaching squarely on the Bible.

Let us hear the conclusion of the matter. Every once in a while, perhaps once a year, there is among Bible-loving Christians a worthy place for a series of expository lectures. The

---

[9] The text would be II Cor. 8:9.
[10] See *George W. Truett, a Biography*, by Powhatan W. James, Macmillan, 1939, pp. 112, 172.

easy way to start is with a short book, such as James, in which the unit of thought is the separate paragraph. As one gains skill and confidence one will dare to fish in deeper waters. In each course the choice of the book should depend a good deal on the present needs of the parish.

In many a parish there is need of teaching in biblical ethics. Perhaps the best way to meet this need is to take the people through a course in First Corinthians. There the practical study of problems which perplex us all today leads up to the beautiful thirteenth chapter, and then to the amazing fifteenth chapter. After this vision of the resurrection body and the life everlasting, there is in the sixteenth chapter a closing message about the Christian use of money, and the old-fashioned grace of friendliness. What an intermingling of heavenly visions and earthly tasks!

CHAPTER VIII

THE CHAPTER SERMON

PREACHING from the chapter is more difficult than anything which we have considered thus far. The increased difficulty is due to the greater length of the passage. On the other hand, if the chapter sermon lives up to its possibilities, it is almost certain to be popular. The appeal is due in part to the layman's familiarity with the chapter. He may not know it well, but he remembers that it was marked in his mother's Bible, and he wishes to find out why she loved it dearly.

Here is a situation which should call out the best that is in the preacher. Can he present the truth of a golden chapter so that henceforth it will mean as much to the layman as it used to mean to his mother? By a golden chapter one means a passage like the one hundred third psalm, or the thirteenth chapter of First Corinthians—a chapter which is by common consent more precious than gold. In view of these facts, the minister ought to be unusually careful about choosing the chapter, and unusually diligent in making ready to preach.

SELECTING THE CHAPTER

Many of the principles which have emerged on previous pages rise to greet us again. Ere long they should become our friends for life! First, one should preach from a golden chapter occasionally. Before one starts out on a course or a series, one should learn how to deal with different sorts of chapters, separately. Whatever the chapter, it should be pure gold.

A good place to begin is the nineteenth psalm. The topic may be, "How God Speaks Today." This subject is of vital concern to every thoughtful man or woman, especially to one who has been schooled in science. "How does God break through, and make himself known?" This is the characteristic question of our time. By way of answer the nineteenth psalm suggests three lines of thought. For the commentator there are only two, but for the preacher there may be three. In a deep sense, the three are one.

The first six verses sing about the Word of God in the sky. In this part of the sermon one can appeal to the layman's love of nature. This is wiser than to mystify him with allusions to the theories of Eddington, Jeans, and Einstein. Albert Einstein is a kind neighbor and friend, but he makes it a rule not to talk about science with a layman. Such conversation might not be kind. Other wise men's theories about "the expanding universe" may be correct, at least "relatively" so; but unless one has both the time and the ability to make any scientific allusion clear, why risk the detour? In a popular sermon it is better simply to explain the nineteenth psalm, which has almost nothing to do with present-day science. The psalm teaches us to sing about God as he makes himself known in the silence of the stars at night. These grand old simplicities of our faith do not change with expanding science.

The next five verses sing about the Word of God in the Bible. One is tempted to take up each successive verse and try to translate it into crude American prose. But why do that? Is not the inspired poet saying the same few things again and again? Does he not appeal to the heart more than to the head? So should this central part of the sermon. It might be well, however, to point out the use of repetition for emphasis, and the love for the concrete word, as well as the vivid phrase. When the layman begins to commit these beautiful words to memory, he will be glad to note the many ways in which the poet says that God is making his glory known through the Bible. As in the first part of the sermon, here also one stresses the fact that God is waiting to make himself known to everyone present. Thus God speaks today, both in the sky and in the Book.

The last three verses sing about the Word of God in the heart. Thus the pattern of the nineteenth psalm differs from that of the one hundred third. In the nineteenth psalm the message of God comes first from the silent stars, then from the open Book, and last of all to the waiting heart. In the longer psalm the melody starts in the soul of the singer, and then gradually soars out into the immensities, until ere long there is a hallelujah chorus of earth and heaven. However, as in a moving sermon, the closing appeal in the one hundred third psalm is to the individual soul. As literature, the nineteenth psalm is not so sublime as the one hundred third. Some day the longer psalm will lead to an expository sermon which the lay hearer will remember with gladness as long as he lives. But while the minister is learning to preach from the chapter, he will find it easier to make clear and luminous the successive stages of the nineteenth psalm.

Again, one should select a chapter with a strong, vital message for today. On the Sunday before Thanksgiving, for instance, or near some other national holiday, one may preach from the eighty-fifth psalm. The subject may be, "Our Nation on its Knees." The first three verses sing about the goodness of God to our nation in the past. The next four are filled with praises for his blessings upon our land today. The last six voice our hope for his mercies in days to come. Throughout the sermon the practical helpfulness will depend largely upon the preacher's ability to discuss these truths concretely, as they concern our beloved land today. Surely the time has come when the preacher should enlighten the people about the Christian interpretation of American history.[1]

Lastly, one should not anticipate any part of a future series. Some of these days one will have a whole series of sermons from golden chapters. A good place to begin one's serial preaching is the Book of Psalms. If the series next summer is likely to include the nineteenth psalm, or the eighty-fifth, it might be well to preach the "exploratory sermon" from a chapter in the New Testament. An easy place to begin is the thirteenth chapter of First Corinthians. The books of reference may include Henry Drummond's *Addresses*,[2] especially the one about love as "The Greatest Thing in the World"; and J. D. Jones's book of sermons, *The Greatest of These*.[3] The real authority, however, is the Apostle Paul, or rather the Holy Spirit. The same Spirit who once spake through Paul is waiting now to speak through the local pastor.

PREACHING ABOUT LOVE

The topic of the sermon may be "The Greatness of Christian

---

[1] For the secular facts see *The Rise of American Civilization*, by Chas. A. and Mary Beard, 3 vols., Macmillan, 1927-39.

[2] H. M. Caldwell Co., New York, n.d., pp. 9-44.

[3] Doran, 1925.

Love." The text is the closing verse of the chapter.[4] The introduction has to do with the popular favor of this prose poem. While the fourteenth chapter of John is the favorite with many of us older people, Paul's "Hymn of Christian Love" is the choice of our sons and daughters. All of us love these golden words. We are glad to hear the first three verses, which tell about Christian love as greater than all other good things on earth. We are still more grateful for the next four verses, which show what Christian love is in itself. We rejoice most of all in the last six verses, which exalt Christian love because it lasts. In committing the chapter to memory it is helpful to note the three ascending stages of thought and feeling.

The first part of the hymn reminds us that Christian love is great by contrast. Paul is contrasting it with five other good things which the "saints" in Corinth looked upon as great: oratory, prophecy, miracle-working, philanthropy, and martyrdom. That is no mean list. But when a man is preaching in Chicago, or Atlanta, why should he not speak in terms of his own city? Why not substitute for Paul's five good things these other five, which the modern man or woman looks upon as great: money, pleasure, health, education, power? In the sermon, however, the emphasis should be upon Christian love, not upon these human substitutes. Christian love is great in the eyes of God. Each of these other things, whether in Corinth or Chicago, is a good gift of the Father's bounty, and may be used in his service. But all five together, or all ten, do not begin to be so great as Christian love. For a lifelong series of object lessons showing how a

---

[4] I Cor. 13:13.

modern university professor has used all of the American five with gusto in the service of his fellow-men, read the *Autobiography with Letters* of William Lyon Phelps.[5] One of many reasons why he has long since mastered the fine art of getting along with people is that early in life he became a "Browningite"; that is, a lover of God and fellow-men, one by one.

The first part of the sermon enables one to present the Christian philosophy of life in terms of love.[6] It is better to do so concretely, as Paul does, than to utter ponderous deliverances about totalitarianism, materialism, and utilitarianism. Why not add "futilitarianism"? Indeed, one might make this New Year's resolution: "By God's grace I shall preach nothing but facts, and keep silent about every 'ism' or 'ology.'" Of course there is a crying need for light upon the pagan philosophies which seem to be in control of the world today. But the average minister is scarcely equipped to explain such things to the average layman. On the other hand, anyone who is called to preach can make clear and luminous the Christian philosophy of life in terms of love.

The central part of the sermon deals with the greatness of Christian love in itself. No one can define it. To define is to set limits, and there are no limits to Christian love. "God is love,"[7] and who can define God? On the human level, however, one can describe love as "the desire for another person when absent; the delight in that person when present."

---

[5] Oxford University Press, 1939, p. 207 *et passim*.
[6] See *Five Great Philosophies of Life*, by William D. Hyde, Macmillan, 1928.
[7] I John 4:8*b*. See the definition of God in the Westminster *Shorter Catechism*, No. 4.

Instead of discussing the apostle's specifications, fifteen in all, one can gather them all up in three sentences, and repeat these sentences often enough to impress them on the hearer's memory. First, "Christian love means being like the Lord Jesus." In fact, one can paraphrase the central part of the chapter by substituting for the word love the name of Jesus: "Jesus suffered long and was kind; he envied not," and so on through verse seven. Second, "Christian love means being a gentleman, or a gentlewoman." Here one should laud the "grand old name of gentleman." Third, "Christian love means being able to get along with people." This is the finest of all the fine arts.

The last part of the chapter shows that Christian love is greatest of all because it endures. The last main part of the sermon should be the best of all, for the chapter leads up to a climax. The order here is that of time. When other good things fade, Christian love endures. In fact, it increases. It waxes stronger and stronger. It keeps increasing from childhood over into manhood. The love which awakens in a baby's heart when he first discovers his mother's smile is not so vast as the love which will flood his soul when he looks upon the face of his first-born son.

Likewise does true love keep increasing from early manhood or womanhood over into old age. Much as love fills the heart of the blushing bride as she breathes her marriage vows, more will it suffuse her soul when she is a grandmother. This may be partly why Browning teaches us to sing in "Rabbi ben Ezra":

"Grow old along with me!
  The best is yet to be,

The last of life, for which the first was made;
Our times are in his hand,
Who saith, 'A whole I planned,
Youth shows but half; trust God; see all; nor be afraid.' "

Best of all, Christian love endures from time over into eternity. Little else lasts beyond the grave. Money does not. If there are no pockets in a shroud, thank God! Have you not had worries enough about money here below? So is it with other good things which are of the earth, earthy. They have their day, and they cease to be. Each of them is a good gift of the Father's bounty, but the blessing does not last. Among all the things that are good, the essence which endures is the spirit of Christian love. In heaven that spirit will have its way. Everybody will love everybody else. Why then fear death? [8] Remember that in the New Testament "the center of gravity is beyond the grave." Listen again to "Rabbi ben Ezra":

"Fool! All that is at all
Lasts ever, past recall;
Earth changes, but thy soul and God stand sure."

LETTING THE SERMON GROW

For our next object lesson we shall take the fifteenth chapter of Luke. While this golden chapter calls for various sermons from specific texts, there is a distinct advantage in preaching about the chapter as a whole. The message is that of the entire Third Gospel, which tells about the beauty of God's redeeming grace. From this high point of view let us look at the fifteenth chapter, so as to bring out a few guiding principles.

---

[8] See "Prospice," by Robert Browning.

First, one should understand the chapter as a whole. In order to do that, one needs to know the Gospel of Luke. Even there, no other chapter so fully expresses the joys of one who wins the soul that is lost. While the chapter contains three parables, the three are one. There is a sort of far-sighted parallelism; the Master says the same thing in three different ways. The emphasis throughout is upon the manifold grace of God. There is emphasis, also, upon the lost sheep, the lost coin, and the lost son.

Second, from the chosen point of view one analyzes the chapter, a paragraph at a time. In Luke fifteen, while one could use each paragraph as the basis for more than a few telling sermons, one should look at each section in relation to the whole chapter. For this purpose one finds the arrangement of the three parables ideal. In the tale about the lost sheep one hears the strong masculine note; in the words about the lost coin, the sweet domestic appeal; in the story of the lost son, the blending of sweetness and strength. Here, then, are unity and order, movement and climax. For one who has the eye to see things large and see them whole, there is in the Bible no more wondrous preaching chapter.

Third, in presenting these materials one should be far more intent on preaching a sermon than on making a detailed exposition. Otherwise, one might get lost in the forest, so as to see nothing but trees. Since popular preaching calls for clear interpretation in the light of a practical purpose, one should select and omit in order to heighten and impress. At every step one should keep in view the controlling purpose. It may be either pastoral or evangelistic. If pastoral, one may use these facts in leading up to an appeal for the Christian hearer to taste the joys of winning the soul that is lost. If evangelistic, one may lead up to the appeal for the hearer to come back home to the heart of the Father God.

If the resulting sermon makes the facts seem simpler than they are in life, that is what the popular interpreter often wishes to do. If he were teaching mathematics he would begin with the grand old simplicities, not with differential calculus. Of course the preacher himself should be at home amid the deep things of God. He should be able to follow the most erudite discussions about "the theological implications of God's redeeming grace." But in the pulpit he should judge his chapter sermon by its "significant simplicity," rather than its "impressive pregnancy." [9]

For an example of a chapter sermon we turn to a volume which is little known.[10] The sermon which appears in outline on the following page is expository in substance, simple in structure, and pleasing in style. It is worthy of study because there is skillful use of parallelism, effective use of repetition for emphasis, and equally effective use of the present tense. Even when the preacher is engaged most directly in expositon, he is evidently striving to meet the needs of the man in the pew.

FINDING THE LOST

Introduction (59 words)—The three parables are one.

I. There are three ways of getting lost. The soul may get
        lost as—

---

[9] See *The Teaching of Jesus,* by H. H. Wendt, transl., Scribner, 1892, I, 139.

[10] *Concerning the Christ,* by John D. Freeman, Cincinnati, n.d., pp. 173-90.

A. The sheep got lost—through heedlessness.
    1. A paragraph of explanation (past tense).
    2. A paragraph of discussion (present tense).
B. The coin got lost—through sluggishness.
    1. A paragraph of explanation (past tense).
    2. A paragraph of discussion (present tense).
C. The son got lost—through willfulness.
    1. A paragraph of explanation (past tense).
    2. A paragraph of discussion (present tense).

II. There are three consequences of getting lost.
    A. The consequence of helpless wretchedness.
    B. The consequence of uselessness.
    C. The consequence of degradation.
        (In each subhead, only a little explanation;
          much discussion, in terms of today.)

III. There is a threefold quest of that which is lost.
    A. The quest of the Christ.
    B. The quest of the Holy Spirit.
    C. The quest of the Heavenly Father.
        (In each subhead, only a little explanation;
          much discussion, in terms of today.)

No formal conclusion. The whole sermon is about the individual.

PREPARING A CHAPTER SERIES

Since people like to hear about familiar chapters, why not prepare a series? As a rule the chapters which people love best are ones that lend themselves readily to sermonic uses. In selecting the chapters it may be wise to let the people help. This idea came to a pastor during his call on a deacon, who was convalescing after an illness. The deacon was committing to memory eight chapters from a list handed out by the seminary professor who had taught the Men's Bible Class. When the pastor found that the other members of the class had welcomed the list of chapters, he decided to ask them for lists of their own favorites. Each list was to include eight chapters, though four might have been a better number.

Through the Men's Class, the bulletin, and by her own efforts, the secretary secured more than a hundred lists. From them she compiled the list of chapters for the series of eight sermons. This way of preaching with the people led to large attendance at the evening service, and to increased love for the Book. The general title of the series was "Golden Chapters in the Bible." These were the topics:

> The Majesty of God's Law (Exod. 20)
> The Goodness of Our Shepherd (Ps. 23)
> The Kindness of the Father (Ps. 103)
> The Sufferings of Our Saviour (Isa. 53)
> The Gospel in the Old Testament (Isa. 55)
> The Joy of Finding the Lost (Luke 15)
> The Secret of the Untroubled Heart (John 14)
> The Practical Life of the Christian (Rom. 12)

It might have been better to ask for favorite chapters from a single book. This is one way of encouraging the people to know the Bible by books. The logical place to start would be the Psalms. The heading might be, "Psalms Our People Love," or in an outdoor series, "Psalms of the Open Air."[11] After the people have grown accustomed to the plan, one may turn to a more difficult field, the Book of Isaiah. The list below includes eight chapters, but it might be better to run two separate series, under the general heading, "Golden Chapters from Isaiah." Fortunately one need not adhere to the chapter divisions:

---

[11] The first list, Pss. 1, 23, 91, 103, 148; the second, Pss. 8, 19, 46, 90, 121.

Let us look at the greatest of these chapters, the fifty-third. In the Hebrew it is a poem with five strophes. Each strophe is one line longer than the last, to show increasing importance. For us Christians the poem is about Christ.[12] The five strophes afford the framework for a message about "Our Suffering Saviour." Ordinarily one prefers less than five main parts. But if there must be that many, each of them should stand out. Five words may be the signposts to guide the layman in this steep ascent to Calvary. These five words follow the principle of alliteration, a device which is proper if the words come of their own accord. Like the use of puns, this other habit grows. Unless one is careful, alliteration may become merely a pulpit trick.

The first strophe presents the Divine Servant.[13] He alone is the Ideal Servant of God and man. The Servant shows that the way to do the will of God on earth is to serve men, one by one. The keynote of the first strophe is, "Behold my Servant." The speaker is God.

The second strophe points to the Divine Sufferer.[14] The speaker appears to be the prophet. The keynote is about Christ: "He was despised, and rejected of men." These words

[12] Cf. Acts 8:35.
[13] Isa. 52:13-15.
[14] Isa. 53:1-3.

dominate the thought early in the second part of Handel's *Messiah*. When Handel arrived at this stage in the composition a friend found him with his head down upon the table. He was weeping, because he had caught a vision of the Cross. Once when the late Bishop Francis W. Warne came home from India, he said that the saddest spectacle in the homeland was that of Christian men and women singing about the Cross, even at the Lord's Supper, with never a catch in the voice or a tear in the eye.

The third strophe shows the Divine Substitute.[15] Here again the speaker appears to be the prophet. He represents heartbroken sinners, of whom he is one. The spirit is that of J. Y. Simpson, at Edinburgh, where he discovered chloroform. After his death friends found that on the margin of his Bible the distinguished scientist had changed each of the personal pronouns to the singular. In the translation which appears below, the order of words is that in the Hebrew, where the emphasis is upon the pronouns. The only alteration is the substitution of the singular. The facts here suggest a sermon about "The Cross in Personal Pronouns." Is there any other kind of Cross?

But he—he was wounded for transgressions that were mine;
He was beaten small for sins that were mine;
The discipline of my peace was upon him;
And because of his stripes there is healing for me.

The fourth part of the poem is the noblest thus far. The strophe exalts the Divine Sacrifice.[16] The speaker is still the prophet. This time he represents sinners who are redeemed.

---

[15] Isa. 53:4-6.
[16] Isa. 53:7-9.

148

The redemption is through sacrifice, a fact which stands out in the key verse: "He is brought as a lamb to the slaughter." The emphasis here, as in the New Testament, is not on what he suffered, but on how, and why. Though he was sinless, yet he suffered in silence; for us men and our salvation was he slain. In our sermons do we keep telling this old, old story, and do we tell it simply, as to a little child? The heart of the Gospel is here. It is here because he who once was slain is now alive, and shall be evermore.

Last of all, and most sublime, is the strophe about the Divine Satisfaction.[17] The reference is not to a well-known dogma of the Church, but to a fact which may be more acceptable to the modern mind. "He shall see of the travail of his soul, and shall be satisfied." The speaker appears to be God. He is telling his redeemed children to think about the Cross in terms of victory, not defeat. The word travail bespeaks inexpressible anguish. But it is the sort of anguish which leads to life for another. In this case there is life for countless others, one by one. Now that our Lord can look back over all that he endured on earth, supremely on the Cross, and likewise look forward to the oncoming triumph of his Kingdom, he is vastly more than satisfied.

What, then, are the satisfactions of suffering? The Cross is the answer. It shows that Christ suffered according to the will of God; that he suffered for others, whom he loved even unto the death; and that through suffering he saved them from sin and woe. Would that everyone whom the loving God permits to suffer might do so with holy satisfaction! Such a spirit of glad acceptance breathes out from almost

---

[17] Isa. 53:10-12.

every part of the New Testament,[18] and likewise from the noblest of our hymns about the Cross. For instance, take these two: "When I survey the wondrous Cross," and "O sacred head now wounded, with grief and shame bowed down." Think, also, about the triumphant song of the Church: "Crown him with many crowns."

PREACHING FROM CHAPTERS IN JOHN

After this series from golden chapters in Isaiah one may do some other sort of preaching for a while. Then one may turn to the Fourth Gospel for a series which will bring the people joy. They will gladly hand in lists of favorite chapters. The choices will vary widely, as there are in this book at least a dozen chapters which call for popular sermons. However, it is wise to keep the numbers down, and then work hard on the chosen few. Fortunately, the chapters which the people love best are ones which a man should be able to present; that is, if he knows the Lord, and if he is willing to "preach suggestively, not exhaustively." Even the simplest chapter in the Fourth Gospel is difficult to fathom. On the other hand, the most refreshing water comes from the deepest well.

The general title of the series may be, "The Book We Love Best," or else, "Golden Chapters from John." This latter title is clearer. In naming a popular series one gives the preference to the title that is clear. The topic of the opening sermon may be, "The Genesis of the Gospel."[19] Both as literature and as a source of spiritual light, the opening chapter in John resembles the first one in Genesis. There the

---

[18] E.g., I Pet. 2:11-25.
[19] John 1:1-18. In verse 14 the second clause means literally, "He tented among us."

majestic record tells how God makes himself known in the Creation. Here the still more majestic record tells how he makes himself known far more wondrously in the mystery of the Incarnation. A mystery is a holy truth which we mortals could never have discovered for ourselves, but which we can learn through God's revelation. The mystery of the Incarnation is that our Lord took up his abode on earth in a human body, as in a tent. Thus he brought the life of God to sinful man, so as to win the heart of man back to God.

The next sermon may be, "The Beginning of the Christian Life." [20] The Christian life begins when one is born from above. The third message has to do with "The Christian Secret of the Abundant Life." [21] By means of a beautiful figure, that of the shepherd, the chapter tells about the Living Christ as our Leader. The fourth sermon may be about the most wonderful chapter in the Bible.[22] This chapter tells about "The Christian Secret of the Untroubled Heart." The secret is faith in the Father, the Son, and the Holy Spirit. In this golden chapter, as in the Apostles' Creed, the emphasis is on what Phillips Brooks calls "the manifold helpfulness of the Triune God." [23] The fifth sermon may be about "The Glory of Religion as Friendship." [24] Religion here is a "deepening friendship" with the Living Christ.

Thus the interpreter can guide his friends into a loving appreciation of golden chapters in the Bible. No other sermons during the year will produce larger dividends in the

---

[20] John 3:1-21.
[21] John 10:1-18.
[22] John 14:1-18.
[23] For popular interpretations of the Trinity, see his *Sermons*, Dutton, 1910, I, 228, and II, 318-35.
[24] John 15:1-17.

way of gratitude. What people can fail to love and thank the friend who leads them into one mountain height after another, and from each new vantage point shows them the glories of earth and sky? But it is not easy to be a mountain guide. Neither is it easy to follow him in the steep ascent to heaven.

When George Adam Smith was young he once climbed a steep ascent in the Alps.[25] Despite the perils, he felt secure, for he was in the care of two strong, skillful guides. One of them went a few steps before, and the other followed closely after. When at last they had scaled the mountain almost to the summit, the leading guide asked the young man to step ahead, that he might behold the waiting glory. Forgetting about the gale which was blowing from the other side of the rocks, the young man leaped up on the ledge, but the chief guide quickly dragged him down, exclaiming, "On your knees, sir! You are not safe here except on your knees!"

---

[25] See his sermons, *The Forgiveness of Sins,* Cincinnati, 1904, p. 87.

CHAPTER IX

THE BIBLE READING

THUS far we have been thinking about preaching in terms of the Lord's Day. Now let us consider the midweek service, which is much less formal. In the typical parish this part of the weekly program is an ever-present problem. At the monthly meeting with the officers, the minister discusses the matter, pro and con, often disconsolately. At the midweek service itself most of the songs are likely to be pitched on a minor key; and the rest of the program, including the prayers, gives the impression of being unprepared. The difficulty seems to be that there is no clearly defined objective, such as there was in one of John Wesley's class-meetings.

Yet the midweek meeting lingers on. If some impatient parson puts it out of the way, his successor is likely to witness its return to life, perhaps under a different name, such as "the fireside service." All the while the minister is scarcely content without some sort of meeting for worship between Sundays. Wherever the midweek service is vital, it meets a real need in the parish. No one has discovered any satisfactory substitute for the prayer meeting. How could one keep the heart of the local church healthy without some opportunity for social worship and quiet readings from the Bible, followed by social fellowship? How then can the minister help to put new life into the old prayer meeting? As a rule the answer comes best in the way of informal worship, with equally informal

153

Bible readings, usually from part of a book in the Bible—and all led by the pastor.

WEDNESDAY EVENING MEETINGS

When the minister first comes into the parish and begins to preach from the Bible, he soon discovers that the people need some other sort of biblical teaching. He thanks God for all the good work which laymen are doing as volunteers in the Bible school; but as he goes on his pastoral rounds, and as he meets with his friends, one by one, in the study, he finds them woefully ignorant of the Scriptures. Some are eager to use the Bible in solving their daily problems, and in thinking about the world at large. At least a few will come out week by week to a fireside service where they can enjoy a season of restful worship, and talk together informally about an interesting portion of the Book. But the man who guides them should be an expert. He should know how to lead in group worship, and how to teach the Bible informally.

Under skillful leadership the attendance should increase, but it may never grow large in proportion to the size of the flock. However, why worry about numbers? "There is no restraint to the Lord to save by many or by few."[1] When Paul met for prayer with the women on the river bank at Philippi, the numbers were few. When he and Silas held an informal meeting at the city jail, the numbers were probably still smaller. But in each case Luke reports a blessing.[2] Today when a pastor is learning how to guide a group in worship, followed by informal conversation about some part of the

---

[1] I Sam. 14:6c; cf. Judg. 7:1-7.
[2] Acts 16:13-15, 25-34.

Bible, numbers might even be an obstacle. At a Sunday morning service everyone feels the inspiration of numbers, but at an informal meeting it is easier to lead a group which is fairly small.

This tendency to keep the numbers down is noteworthy in present-day education. Five miles from us at Lawrenceville School, where hundreds of boys are preparing for the university under the Harkness Plan, each recitation group is small. At Princeton University, where Woodrow Wilson introduced the preceptorial plan, the professor's lecture is followed by meetings in small groups. The value of the small "precept" depends on the skill of the leader, but so does the value of the preceding lecture vary with the ability of the professor. In the Graduate School a class of eight is considered large enough; the number may be smaller. At the Institute for Advanced Study this year Albert Einstein is responsible for the oversight of two men. At the Seminary, also, we are seeking for ways of breaking up into sections more than one class of sixty men. At the Westminster Choir College much the same condition prevails. Whatever the institution, if the class is large, the teacher is tempted to do all the talking. For much the same reason, the class session tends to become formal. In view of these facts, why should the leader of the midweek service keep harping about numbers?

There is no fool-proof way of conducting such a meeting, but a few facts are obvious. One is that when the minister is within the bounds of the parish he should be present at every meeting. Whenever he is present he should lead. In a teaching service continuity of leadership counts strongly. Whenever the pastor is to lead, he plans every detail with care. He is present fifteen minutes before the time, and he has everything in readiness. He arranges with the organist and the song leader to start the meeting when the clock strikes eight. During the first twenty-five minutes the pastor leads the informal worship. If the people have been standing at their work throughout the day, he lets them remain seated while they sing. Likewise during the twenty-five minutes that he sets apart for the Bible reading he plans that everyone except himself shall remain seated. The pastor seldom sits down, except at a cottage meeting. If he stands he is better able to keep the service moving. He manages always to be through in less than sixty minutes.

Again, the minister should know how to lead. The true pastor is a skillful leader. The word pastor means shepherd. The shepherd's business is to lead. In conducting the worship of a small group, and in teaching them, a platform or a pulpit would be a handicap; a stand or a little table is better. On it should be a watch, which is accurate, and sure to keep running. There should be nothing else except the Bible and the hymn book. Throughout the sixty minutes, one or the other of these books should be in the leader's hands almost continuously. As he faces the people—who are sitting close together, and near the pastor—on his right hand is the piano, and on his left is the blackboard. Thus the furnishings of the room suggest worship and teaching, as the two foci round which everything moves. A little later, both of them should give way to old-fashioned friendliness. People who love the Lord should love each other. As for getting the people together at a supper before the meeting, such a plan should work well where it ought to work at all. What concerns us now is that both in worship and teaching the minister should guide his friends with contagious enthusiasm.

Once more, during the latter half of the hour the focus should be the Bible, not the minister. The idea is to show the layman how to read the Bible, not to show how much the pastor knows about it. The stress is on how to enjoy the Bible, not on how to swallow it as medicine, in doses large or small.[3] Most of our people endure the Bible, or else give it "absent treatment." Seldom do they respond to fervent appeals for "Bible study." They look upon study as work. However mistakenly, they think they already have work enough, perhaps too much. They come to church to enjoy themselves. If they do not relish what they get, they quit coming. They wish the minister to study the Bible. That is partly why they pay him! As for themselves, they would prefer simply to read the Word as their guidebook in everyday living. But they scarcely know how! They wish that the minister would show them how to enjoy reading the Bible. Except in an unusual parish, such as the one which appears at the end of this chapter, it seems wise to say little about Bible study, and much about Bible reading. Bible study is like doctrinal preaching; the reality is far more popular than the name.

READINGS FROM PHILIPPIANS

It is good to begin with a short, easy book. For instance, take Philippians. It lends itself admirably to a course of Bible readings during the autumn, when one is laying the foundations for the year's work in the parish. Through the bulletin

---

[3] See Anthony C. Deane, *How to Enjoy the Bible,* Doran, 1925; and Julian P. Love, *How to Read the Bible,* Macmillan, 1940.

one announces the course of reading, and asks each person who attends to bring a Bible. Since much of the reading is to be in concert, everyone should have the same version. Usually it is the King James. In the meeting one says little about method; that would sound like work. Still one makes it clear that the Bible was written by books, and that the way to know it is to read it, a book at a time, much as young people in high school come to know Shakespeare. Instead of racing through all that he wrote, and priding themselves on the number of times they have read Shakespeare "straight through from cover to cover," our sons and daughters do not read on a merry-go-round. They take up one play at a time, perhaps beginning with *Henry the Fifth*. They read it more than once, part by part, until they know it as a friend. Why should not the layman learn how to love his Bible, book by book, and part by part?

The general subject for the course may be, "Bible Readings from Philippians." At the first meeting the pastor introduces the book to his friends. He talks about it lovingly as William Lyon Phelps would do in presenting Browning's masterpiece, *The Ring and the Book,* or Bliss Perry with Emerson's *Essays.* In commending the Bible book as a whole, one need not outline it for the people; that would smack of study. Rather should one describe it as a love letter from Paul to the congregation which was closest to his heart. When he wrote this loving letter he was lonely and frail, penniless and in prison, facing death for his Saviour's sake. Nevertheless, Paul was happy. He was radiant. This letter is the most joyous part of the New Testament, where joy abounds. What, then, is "The Christian Secret of Joy"? The Epistle to the

Philippians is the answer. What a book for a day when the world is in turmoil!

In successive meetings one takes up the book by paragraphs, consecutively, in the light of the controlling purpose. In preparing for any meeting, one decides whether to keep to a single paragraph, or take a small cluster. But one's program must be elastic. The people may wish to linger longer than one expects, or else not so long. In any case, one tries to keep each paragraph intact. All of this may sound like old-fashioned expository lecturing. So it is, in substance, but not in form. Instead of serving formally as the speaker of the house, the minister is the leader of a lively discussion group.

INFORMAL CONVERSATION

The idea is for the people to talk. But no one should speak unless he has something to say. If two or three of the older laymen persist in making long prayers, and still longer talks, even while sitting down, the minister should secretly confer about the matter with the Lord, and then hold a personal interview with each loquacious brother, explaining to him the desire for friendly conversation, with its give and take, and not for any monologue, however helpful. If any brother should feel so ashamed as to absent himself for a week or two, doubtless the meeting would survive that long without him. In short, leadership calls for tact!

A worthy leader knows how to listen. He knows that every paragraph in Philippians suggests more than a few questions, and that anyone present can ask a question. When it comes, the leader can get others to answer, not exhaustively, but suggestively. Thus the spirited talk moves back and forth from pastor to layman much as a tennis ball keeps crossing the net. Once in a while the ball may drop to the ground, but the master of tennis knows how to keep the ball in play. Now, as in Paul's time, we Christians should speak about religion in terms of play as well as work.[4] Most of us enjoy a game, especially when we take part. Still more do we enjoy spirited conversation, in which everyone is free to listen or to speak. As the good woman said to the neighbor who asked if she had enjoyed the meeting the night before, "Of course I did; I took part three times!"

The leader, also, should enjoy every minute. In a high sense, being happy is the minister's chief business here below, especially in days of distress. Living as he does amid many people who are not happy, he should show them what it means to be a Christian.[5] Why be as solemn as the wrong sort of mortician, with his professional parade of piosity? Especially when one is considering "The Christian Secret of Joy," one should be radiant. As William Lyon Phelps often says, "The happiest person is the one who thinks the most interesting thoughts."[6]

Occasionally, however, enthusiastic informality leads to a delicate situation. Once in the olden days a young parson was taking his people through the Book of Malachi, which tells about "An Old-Fashioned Revival." This book teaches that when God's people get right with him they gladly pay the

---

[4] See Phil. 2:16; 3:14; Heb. 12:1; also *The Metaphors of St. Paul*, by J. S. Howson, London, 1868.
[5] Phil. 4:4-7.
[6] *Autobiography with Letters*, Oxford University Press, 1939, p. 931.

tithe, or more, and that through the Church.[7] During the
animated discussion of this paragraph one of the men, forgetting that tithing originally came from God, asked the
minister, "Is it fair to the working-man?" In that parish
there was only one day-laborer. He had six children, none
of them large. Since he was earning only $1.50 a day, he
was quietly receiving aid from the deacons. Fortunately, he
was not present at the meeting. Without pausing to get his
bearings, the young parson replied, "If I were earning only
$1.50 a day, and had to provide for a wife and six children, I
do not see how we could pay the tithe."

Then he might have related the following, which is true.
In the Middle West fifty years ago a pastor died leaving a
widow with five growing children. She took them to a
little farm which she had inherited. After six months of
hopeless struggle to make ends meet, she called the older
children together and told them: "When your father was with
us we always paid the tithe. Since I have been in charge, I
have quit. Now I wish to start again, if you are willing."

"Why, Mother, we cannot live on ten-tenths; how can we
get along on nine?"

"Children, I believe that nine-tenths with God's blessing
will go further than ten-tenths is going now. Let us all
pray about it."

The children responded to their mother's spirit. Working
and giving as laborers together under God they grew up in
a home where he was the chief partner. Two of them rose
to distinction in the Church, and each of the others added
luster to the family name. In after years one of them told

[7] Mal. 3:7-12.

a group of friends that he had become a minister and a missionary largely because his mother had honored her God with money.

"But this sort of informality must require a vast deal of time! How long will it take to deal with Philippians?" Probably eight or ten weeks. Perhaps six would be better. Instead of stopping to admire each verse, as though it were an unset diamond, one encourages the friends to look at the Bible in a larger way. In each paragraph one makes the distinctive truth stand out. A good way to do that is to use the blackboard. It helps one to secure variety, and also to stress what is essential. While one is writing, one should not talk, at least not much. By watching motion pictures one should see the wisdom of synchronizing what attracts the eye with what appeals to the ear. Whatever goes on the board should be as brief and striking as the script in a first-class motion picture. For example, in dealing with Paul's words about "The Christian Secret of Contentment," [8] one may write out the following words and then have the people read them aloud, in concert, more than once: "Live without worry. Work without hurry. Look forward without fear." Surely our people should be able to learn these lessons from Philippians without stealing away to the Wednesday evening meeting at the Christian Science Church.

"But what about the difficult passages?" In Philippians there is only one. That is in the second chapter, the opening paragraph.[9] Doctrinally, these words about the Incarnation

---

[8] Phil. 4:10-13. In the Greek the three dominant verbs are especially significant.
[9] Phil. 2:1-11.

bristle with difficulties. Practically, they teach that "the mind of Christ" calls for humility, service, and sacrifice. As an object lesson one may use Albert Schweitzer. He gladly relinquished a brilliant career in philosophy, theology, or music, in order to become a missionary doctor in Africa. But what a doctor, and what a missionary! [10]

"At the end of eight weeks, what will the people know about the book?" They will know little about Philippi as a Roman colony, and less about the kenotic theories of the Incarnation. But they should know that the secret of joy in hard times is through loving fellowship with the Living Christ, as he shines out through every part of this little letter. Likewise should they know the epistle itself, and be able to use it in any hour of need. Especially should they know by heart the most precious passages. These occur chiefly in the fourth chapter. It is full of pure gold.

The following outline shows the basic framework of what one minister has discovered in the Epistle to the Philippians. Starting with the fact that Paul founded this church during his second missionary journey, and that he wrote the epistle during his second Roman imprisonment, the minister has learned that this letter shows how to be happy when times are hard.

THE CHRISTIAN SECRET OF JOY

I. The Joys of the Christian Believer (Phil. 1).
   A. Praying for Others (vv. 3-11).
      1. Thanksgiving. 2. Petition.
   B. Trusting in God (12-20).

---

[10] See *Out of My Life and Thought*, Henry Holt, 1933.

1. Providence. 2. The Church. 3. Oneself.
C. Living in Hope (21-26).
   1. Philosophy of Life. 2. Dilemma. 3. Decision.

II. The Joys of Christian People (Phil. 2).
   A. Christian Ideals (vv. 1-11).
      1. Humility. 2. Service. 3. Sacrifice.
   B. Christian Habits (12-18).
      1. Work. 2. Radiance. 3. Sacrifice.
   C. Christian Leaders (19-30).
      1. Ministerial. 2. Lay.

III. The Joys of Christian Progress (Phil. 3).
   A. In terms of Business (vv.1-11).
      1. Assets. 2. Liabilities. 3. Profits.
   B. In terms of Athletics (12-16).
   C. In terms of Walking (17-21).

IV. The Joys of Christian Living (Phil. 4).
   A. In Right Relations (1-9).
      1. Others. 2. Oneself. 3. The Lord.
   B. Christian Contentment (10-20).
      1. Acceptance. 2. Learning. 3. Power.

Conclusion: The Secret is "in Christ."

A spirited service of Bible reading and conversation appeals to men as well as women. In a normal parish the minister can judge his ability to lead on Wednesday evening by the proportion of men who come regularly. As the weeks go by, more than one thoughtful layman will remark to his neighbor: "I never knew that reading the Bible could be so enjoyable and helpful." "Yes," the other will reply, "the Bible is becoming a new book. I wonder which part we shall take up next. I hope it will be Romans or else Hebrews."

Either of those epistles might prove too long and too hard. While the sheep are getting accustomed to something strange, it may be wise to feed them in a small pasture, and then shift them soon. The main thing is to be sure that the food is inviting and abundant.

During the progress of the year the readings should afford wholesome variety. After the Christmas holidays one may have a course about personal work, and after Easter a course about missions. Again, there may be a course about trusteeship or else worship. For each meeting there should be a definite passage. It should be clearly stated at the previous meeting and in the bulletin the Sunday before the actual discussion.

In popular teaching of the Scriptures it is wise to single out some one paragraph, or cluster of related paragraphs. Thus one tends to focus the attention of the layman. Instead of confusing him by playing hop-skip-and-jump, let every reading be a unit. When one is leading in a course about missions, or money, one can seldom choose all the successive weekly passages from a single book. In the long run, however, the most profitable course will prove to be that in which the people look at the Bible as it was written, a book at a time. For example, prepare a course of readings from First John, or First Peter.

A worthy course does far more for the pastor than for any of his people. He has to put more in; so he gets more out. He finds that the best way for him to master the Bible is to teach it. Among the many by-products of his studies for these Bible readings, none delights him more than the constantly increasing supply of materials for future sermons. For instance, if he ever wishes to preach from Philippians, as he often should, he will find waiting in his files all sorts of interesting and helpful materials.

For an object lesson of how the plan sometimes operates, turn to Clarence E. Macartney's volume, *Peter and His Lord*.[11] The brief Foreword contains this note about the book: "The ground for these sermons was first broken at the Wednesday Night Service. Some years afterwards, these preliminary sketches were developed into a series of sermons preached at the Sunday morning service."

HOLLYWOOD BIBLE STUDY PLAN

One of the most unusual ways of promoting Bible reading through the midweek service is that of the Hollywood Presbyterian Church, where Stewart P. MacLennan is pastor. The membership in 1939 was 2,411, with a Sunday school enrollment of 3,398. In addition to the meeting described below, there is on Wednesday evening an equally large and enthusiastic gathering of young people, whose social life centers in the church. They too enjoy getting better acquainted with the Bible, and with each other. From this congregation nine young men are now enrolled in our seminary. One of our recent graduates secured the following report from his father, who is a ruling elder in the Hollywood Church:

We have from two hundred to two hundred fifty people present each Wednesday evening. They are divided up into groups of ten around a table. Supper is served at 6:30; it costs forty cents. The pastor selected twenty or twenty-five of the most active men in the church, with a few women, and asked us to serve as "hosts" at the various tables. He urged

---

[11] Cokesbury, 1937, p. 5.

the hosts go out and bring in people who were not attending the midweek meeting. Thus each host, with his wife, makes up his own table, and serves as leader. During the week he tries to get well acquainted with his group personally. In a sense he is their pastor.

Mrs. Cook and I started out from scratch, with nobody at our table. Soon we had the required ten; in fact, we often have twelve or fourteen. We have a lot of fun at the table, cracking jokes and kidding each other. (This of course depends upon the type of leader at each table.) Everybody wants to come back the next week.

The supper is finished shortly after seven o'clock. Then the pastor calls us to order, and a young man leads us all in a few hymns. The pastor makes any brief announcements that he thinks necessary, and perhaps gives a short "pep talk." Some elder or visiting minister leads in prayer. Then there is a short season of silent prayer, during which everyone is to ask for God's blessing upon the service. There is also a short, audible prayer by each leader at his own table. Now comes the period for the Bible reading.

First the members of the group read the assigned chapter, going round the table, with everyone reading a single verse. Then the host tries to get each person to tell the key verse, his favorite verse, and the five most important facts in the chapter. All of this is decidedly informal. Some of us inject a little humor occasionally. We are amazed at the number of original ideas reported every week by these untrained laymen who have been reading the chapter at home again and again. They seem to be having the time of their lives.

Exactly at eight o'clock the minister calls for the reports. The host from each table comes forward in his turn and reads the findings of his group. After every host has reported, the pastor reads his own paper. He too gives the key verse, his favorite verse, and the five chief points about the chapter. Then he comments about any report which he considers unusually good. He seems to think that some of the points brought out by the laymen are as interesting and helpful as any that he himself offers. When he has concluded this part of the program, we laymen surely have a clear idea of what is in the chapter!

We started with the Book of Acts, and finished it in twenty-eight weeks. Then we were going to take up John. Some of us wanted to try Romans, but our pastor thought it might be a little deep. However, it was decided that we should all vote on the book to read next, and Romans it was! We have been at it now for nine weeks, and we are thrilled. Partly through this plan, outside people have become interested, and have confessed their faith in Christ.

As it appears from a distance, the Hollywood Plan affords untold possibilities. In a modified form it would suit the needs of almost any parish, however small. If every pastor and his lay friends would devote such attention to this "problem," they would find that the midweek service is really an opportunity to enjoy getting acquainted with the Bible, book after book.

CHAPTER X

THE BOOK SERMON

W E now turn to the most difficult kind of biblical preaching, except when a man gives a popular bird's-eye view of the Bible as a whole, and that we shall not attempt. Once in a while it is good for both people and pastor to have a sermon which introduces a book of the Bible. For a number of years Harris E. Kirk of Baltimore had his annual series of Sunday evening book sermons. Of course the books were from the Bible. Instead of running the sermons consecutively, he would have one a month, for six months. If he kept up this sort of preaching for eight years, with forty-eight sermons in all, he could present every biblical book which calls for such treatment. The idea is to combine the two books of Samuel, or Kings, which have been divided solely for convenience. One need not devote a sermon to such a minor book as Obadiah or Nahum. The rule is, keep to the main highway.

Another teaching minister preaches a book sermon whenever he is about to launch a course or a series based on the book in hand. The idea is that of the astronomer, such as Henry Norris Russell, at Princeton University, in preparing his friends for what they are about to see on a starry night as they look at the rings of Saturn through the telescope. Thus in time the pulpit interpreter can help his lay friends to know the Bible as it was written, book by book. That is more than the average graduate of the divinity school used to know, when it was the practice for the student to "master the Bible" by listening to the professor lecture about it, and when it was the custom of the professor largely to ignore the way in which the Bible was written.

SELECTING THE BOOK

In choosing the book about which one is to preach as a whole, one ought to be even more careful than in choosing the paragraph or the chapter which is to be the basis of the sermon. Whatever the size of the passage, however, much the same principles obtain. As the unit of thought gets larger, and more complex, the difficulty of handling the materials increases. Here again the secret of popular effectiveness is largely in omitting many things of interest and value in order to present the book as a whole from a single point of view. In other words, the aim is to preach a helpful, uplifting sermon, and not to dissect a part of the Bible in order to display the bones.

It is wise to begin with one of the easy books. Certain books of the Bible lend themselves readily to sermonic treatment; others do not. Of course every minister should start where he can work best. No teacher or lecturer can tell anyone except himself which book to select first. In making the choice the pastor gives special heed to the interests of his people, and to their practical needs. Instead of trying to get the people interested in what attracts him, he prefers to present the book which will help them most in solving their personal problems. He is careful, also, to take up a book which he is able to handle with ease and grace.[1]

---

[1] For a series of popular book studies see *Keynote Studies in Keynote Books of the Bible,* by C. Alphonso Smith, Revell, 1919.

In the Old Testament one of the shortest and easiest books to deal with as a whole is Ruth. Not only is the narrative simple and charming; as the basis of a popular sermon the book presents few difficulties. The Book of Esther, while longer and more complicated, likewise affords excellent preaching ground. Here the subject of the book sermon may be, "The Power of a Good Woman." One may begin with the words of C. Alphonso Smith, formerly professor of English at the University of Virginia: Esther is "the best told story in the Bible."[2] The sermon as a whole should be timely in a day when we all are dismayed by repeated persecutions of the Jews.

Among the prophetic books the difficulties are greater. On the other hand, the field is richer. While every prophetic book is difficult to present as a whole, the undertaking is worth more than it costs. The secret of popular effectiveness is largely in fixing attention on the man rather than the book. The aim is to show how God uses a chosen personality in revealing his holy will to men and nation. What congregation would not welcome a popular introduction to any prophetic book which the pastor knows well enough to make its central message luminous?

By common consent the prophetic books are among the most precious in the Bible. On the other hand, they are the least likely to be understood by the layman. For instance, one day the parson was preaching about heavenly recognition. He insisted that in the other world we shall not only recognize those whom we have known and loved on earth; we shall likewise know and love the men of the Bible, such as Hosea

---

[2] *Op. cit.*

and Amos. The next day one of the deacons said to the minister: "Don't you think it will be embarrassing for me to meet the Minor Prophets and have to confess that I never have read one of their books? I wish that you would tell us how to read Amos and Hosea."

The pastor in turn prepared a series of evening sermons about selected prophets, and later sent these sermons forth in a book for laymen.[3] Among the prophetic books the minister found Amos the easiest to present in a popular way, and Hosea the most appealing. He wonders why he did not include Jonah, and how he ever dared in a single thirty-minute sermon to deal with the entire Prophecy of Isaiah. As for these Major Prophets—the ones whose books are long—they yield their riches most readily to the man who preaches from selected chapters, or other passages which are comparatively short. The fact remains that the minister should guide his people into an intelligent appreciation of the prophetic books, one by one.

In the New Testament, the easiest of the Gospels to present as a whole is Mark. The most pleasing is perhaps Luke. In either case one tries to do much as Charles G. Osgood of Princeton University recently did at the Seminary. On successive days he lectured about Dante's *Inferno,* Spenser's *Faery Queen,* Milton's *Paradise Lost,* and Boswell's *Life of Johnson.* The idea is to tell enough about the author and his book to arouse interest, and to show the hearer what to look for, so that he will determine to read it for himself. Because of the pastor's sermon and the consequent reading of

---

[3] *The Prophets: Elijah to Christ,* by Andrew W. Blackwood, Revell, 1917.

the book, its central message should ever after shine in the layman's soul as a new revelation of God's holy will.

The Book of Acts, also, presents comparatively few difficulties. One looks upon it as "The Acts of the Holy Spirit," or else, "The Acts of the Living Christ." In preaching about the first part of the book, one shows how the Spirit built up the Church largely through the ministry of Peter; in the second main part, chiefly through the ministry of Paul.[4] In each hemisphere there are three grand divisions, which in turn show the founding of the Church, the extension, and the transfer to another city as the center of world Christianity. Thus the emphasis in the sermon, as in Acts, is on evangelism and missions.

Among the epistles, "The last shall be first." The easiest of all to present in a popular message is Philemon, which reveals the heart of the Apostle Paul at his best. The topic may be, "The Religion of a Gentleman." While no other epistle is so simple and so delightfully human, it is not hard to preach about Philippians or First John, James or First Peter. In First Peter, as in many another major book of the Bible, the purpose of the inspired author is to bring strength and hope to a people who are having a hard time. Hence the topic may be "The Religion of Hope"; or, from a different point of view, "The Meaning of Religion as Grace."

Instead of thinking further about separate books, and about paths of approach to them as preaching units, let us turn to three as object lessons. Two are from the Old Testament;

---

[4] Acts 1-11, 13-28; chap. 12 is transitional. For a commentary see R. B. Rackham, *The Acts of the Apostles*, Gorham, New York, 1912.

one is from the New. They should afford examples of how to secure variety among book sermons.

BEGINNING WITH RUTH

In preaching from the Book of Ruth the subject may be, "The Meaning of Religion as Loyalty," or else "Religion in Our Village." The text is the key verse of the book.[5] The introduction may be to look at this simple tale through the eyes of Benjamin Franklin. Once when he was in Paris, at a gathering where the élite of France were making sport of the Bible, he asked the privilege of reading aloud a short story. Throughout the reading they all listened with breathless interest, and then they insisted that he tell them where he had unearthed that exquisite story. He told them that he had been reading the Book of Ruth from the Bible.

In the sermon proper one may show that this young woman lived in a rough and bloody time,[6] much like that through which many a comely young widow has recently been passing in one of the weaker nations of Europe. Over against the black background of domestic grief and prevailing famine, in an atmosphere laden with race prejudice, this little book shows how the grand old simplicities of religion can survive and flourish in the life of a rural community, and especially in the hearts of three human beings whom to know is to love.

While one is reading this little book, one scarcely knows whether to admire most the young woman who was an immigrant, the shrewd mother-in-law who watched over the

---

[5] Ruth 1:16, 17. See also "The Ode to a Nightingale," by John Keats, stanza 7.

[6] Assuming that Ruth and Judges have to do with the same era, read *Israel's Iron Age,* by Marcus Dods, Doran, n.d.

younger woman with ceaseless concern, or the country gentleman who was to become her husband and the father of her
babe. All the while one should keep clearly in view the
central idea which binds the various parts of the book together. That central idea is loyalty. With Ruth, as with each
of us, the cause which inspired loyalty was the Kingdom of
God. But for her that Kingdom first had its being in the
life of a woman who was a daily example of what it means
to trust in God.

Thus the sermon begins to assume its final shape. In the
first main part one can show that true religion expresses
itself in the home. Here the stress is upon the loyalty of a
good young woman to a good older woman. Ordinarily one
preaches in terms of man, rather than woman, but in Ruth
one finds a living object lesson of what is best in either woman
or man—the devotion of heart to heart. Incidentally one can
point out the fact that the mother-in-law who is most prominent in the Bible is worthy of the loyalty which she inspires
in the heart of her daughter-in-law. Such personal loyalty
is close to the center of all true religion.

In the second main part of the sermon one can deal with
the loyalty of a good woman to a good man. Here the horizon
is somewhat broader. In the first part one is thinking chiefly
in terms of the home, and of the intimate relations which
bring out either the best or the worst in a woman. Now one
begins to think rather about the man who is worthy to be the
husband of a woman like Ruth. If in this part of the sermon
one paints an ideal picture of life as it should be in a village
where God has his way, is it not the high privilege of the
minister to hold up community ideals of justice, good will,

and happiness? [7] Would that in Europe today, as in the homeland, every rural community were as nearly ideal as Bethlehem seems to have been in the days of Ruth.

The last part of the sermon is the most vital, and the most difficult to prepare. Here one deals with the loyalty of a good woman to her God. Through loyalty to an older woman there is born in the heart of the daughter-in-law an increasing loyalty to God. "Thy God shall be my God." The spirit of loyalty seems to have dominated the heart of Ruth as she became a wife and a mother. In Hebrew history she became known as the ancestress of King David, and of the Lord Jesus.

The sermon as a whole affords a beautiful opportunity to preach about the local village community in terms of Bethlehem. If one dwells in a city where foreign-born people abound, the emphasis may be upon the way in which God blessed this daughter of an alien land. In either case the sermon will be timely early in December. If on the following Sunday one preaches about Micah, "The Prophet of the Common People," with special reference to what God says about Bethlehem, [8] the people will learn to think about the coming of Christ to their own community, and then they will gladly join in singing:

> "O holy Child of Bethlehem,
> Descend to us, we pray;
> Cast out our sin, and enter in;
> Be born in us today." [9]

PREACHING ABOUT JONAH

It is easier to prepare a sermon about the Book of Ruth

---

[7] Note especially Ruth 2: 4.
[8] Mic. 5:2.
[9] "O Little Town of Bethlehem," by Phillips Brooks, 1868.

than about the Book of Jonah. On the other hand, it is possible to bring forth from this latter book a message even more vital for our day. In an era when practically every land is filled with race prejudice and countless other forms of anti-social godlessness, when the Church of Christ seems to be losing her zeal for the salvation of the world, and when even the best of God's children is tempted to live and work chiefly for self, not for the Kingdom—in such an era there surely is a call for preaching from the Book of Jonah.

"This is the tragedy of the Book of Jonah, that a book which is made the means of one of the most sublime revelations on truth in the Old Testament should be known to most only for its connection with a whale." These words quoted by George Adam Smith [10] suggested to a young pastor the startling subject, "The Book of Jonah: Is the Whale the Hero?" The introduction was in line with the topic, and with the text.[11] The resulting sermon, like the text, had to do with the love of God for the heathen city, and for the unsaved world.

In the first part of a sermon about Jonah one can deal with the provincial prophet as he represents the attitude of the modern man toward world-wide missions. When the prophet was called to preach at Nineveh, he fled in the opposite direction as fast and as far as he could go. If in his mad flight he could have paused to formulate his excuses he might have said what many an objector to missions has been saying in recent days: "I am needed here at home. There is no precedent for my going to that awful city. It would be useless

[10] *The Expositor's Bible*, six-vol. ed., Hartford, 1907, IV, 679*b*.
[11] Jonah 4:11.

for me to go. What could I accomplish single-handed in a city as vast and vile as Nineveh? The plain fact is that I am afraid to go. That city is cruel and bloodthirsty. Then, too, down in my heart I hate Nineveh." This "unloving exclusiveness" is the antithesis of the Christian spirit.[12]

In the second part of the sermon one has to do with the Loving God. He loves the prophet, and calls him to a holy ministry. The Lord follows Jonah to sea and brings him back to give him another opportunity. This same God loves the most wicked city in all the earth, especially the children, and even the cattle. In fact, he loves the whole wide world, in its every race, its every nation, its every class. Where else save in the New Testament can one find a more vivid portrayal of God's "all-embracing love"?

The third part deals with the saved city. Under God, as goes the modern city, thus goes the modern world. According to the Book of Jonah the city of Nineveh is saved by preaching. The preaching is in the spirit of William Booth: "Preach damnation with the Cross in the center." The city is saved by repentance. But, alas, the city is not saved permanently. For instance, where is Babylon, with the glory of her hanging gardens? What once was counted one of the seven wonders of the world is now the scene of desolation—a silent reminder that a city may be spared for a time, and then go down to ruin because of her sins.

The last part of the sermon may seem to be anti-climactic, but in a sense this part is the most practical. Here one deals with the penitent prophet. In modern terms, he is converted

---

[12] For a whimsical description of the provincial attitude see in *The Essays of Elia*, by Charles Lamb, "Imperfect Sympathies."

to enthusiastic belief in foreign missions. He shows his faith by his works. Where previously he may have felt about the people of Nineveh as the Armenian felt about the Turks, that they were created "to people hell with," now Jonah is humble in the hands of God, and is ready to preach at Nineveh. After he preaches he is taught to rejoice because the city is spared from destruction.

Some such transforming experience should come to any modern pastor who does not believe in world-wide missions. When once the pastor begins to share the love of God for the world which is lying under the curse of sin, then the pastor's new-born zeal will begin to spread among the people. One of the best ways to communicate zeal for the extension of the Kingdom throughout the world is to preach the Word. A good place to find material for the sermon is the Book of Jonah.

INTRODUCING FIRST JOHN

The First Epistle of John is less dramatic than the Book of Jonah. In fact, the New Testament as a whole is less dramatic than the Old. In the epistle the emphasis is upon Christian ideas, not upon a vivid personality. The letter has to do with truths, not with action. But this latter book also has a message which should warm the heart. According to Bishop Westcott in his well-known commentary,[13] the dominant truth here is that of fellowship. According to a most suggestive work which is not well known, First John has to do with *The Tests of Life*.[14] In the treatment which follows, the subject is largely from Westcott, but the line of

---

[13] *The Epistles of St. John*, London, 1892.
[14] By Robert Law, Edinburgh, 1914.

thought is more nearly that of Law. Of course the truths themselves are from First John.

The introduction to the sermon has to do with the topic, "The Glory of Christian Fellowship." [15] In the Greek the word translated fellowship means "that which we have in common" with other persons. According to the epistle, our fellowship is with God in Christ, and with those who love the Father God. Fortunately the First Epistle is "catholic," with no local color. Thus, it holds up the ideal of the Christian Church as the most inclusive fellowship on earth.

> "In Christ there is no East or West,
> In him no South or North;
> But one great fellowship of love
> Throughout the whole wide earth." [16]

In the epistle a few main ideas recur again and again, as in a fugue melody. The first of these dominant ideas is that of fellowship with God in light.[17] Light is a symbol of spiritual splendor. God is light, and in him is no darkness; that is, no sin. Through God as he makes his glory known in Christ we sinful mortals find our way into the holy fellowship. We also find the pathway by which we can escape from the bewitching influence of the world. Thank God for light!

The central part of the sermon is about fellowship with God in love.[18] The last main part is about fellowship with God in victory.[19] The victory is over the world, a victory that is wrought through prayer. Thus the sermon proper closes

---

[15] The text is I John 1:3.
[16] John Oxenham, 1908.
[17] I John 1, 2.
[18] I John 3, 4.
[19] I John 5.

with victory over sin. Needless to say, such victory is as remote from the triumphs which we associate with war as light is removed from darkness, or heaven from hell. Throughout the first Epistle of John the tone color is spiritual. That is one reason why it is difficult to preach the sermon. But what parish today does not need the message?

Thus we have thought about preaching from three of the shorter, simpler books of the Bible. By this time the reader has doubtless decided which book he personally can use best as the basis for a popular sermon. That is the book with which he should begin. As he gains skill and confidence he can take up other books, each of them harder than the one before. If he prepares a number of book sermons every year—either in a series or separately—in time he should be able to introduce almost any book in the Bible. Thus he will gradually lead his people to know and love the Bible as it was written, book by book.

At the end of his days in the active ministry he will find that no other sermons have been more rewarding, both to people and pastor.

CHAPTER XI

THE SERMON'S GROWTH

LET us now consider the bearing of
all these facts upon the growth of the sermon for next Sunday
morning. Of course the message should be in the preacher's
mind for weeks before he lets it assume its completed form,
but we are to consider the final stages in the growth of the
sermon.

In its form a sermon from the Bible ought to be like any
other first-class sermon. Whenever the man in the pulpit
interprets the Bible with skill, the man in the pew should
think about the message, not the exposition. Thus the layman should carry home a new revelation of truth. Throughout the week he should live in its blessed light. He will be
able to do so if the sermon is a practical means to a worthy
end. When the passage is from the Old Testament, the
sermon should live and move and have its being in a realm
where God alone is King. If the message is from the New
Testament, the aim should be to bring every thought into
captivity to Jesus Christ. Thus should the minister satisfy the
hearts which keep yearning, "Sir, we would see Jesus."

What, then, is the secret of pulpit effectiveness? The major
sources of preaching power are spiritual. Hence they lie far
beyond the reach of homiletics. Among them all perhaps the
most vital is the mysterious fact of Inspiration. In a fashion all
its own, the Bible has come from God. But fortunately a
man's effectiveness in the pulpit does not depend upon his

theory of Inspiration. F. W. Robertson's ideas here were more liberal than Alexander McLaren's. But many who agree with McLaren wish that they had Robertson's power to preach from the Book. Instead of quarreling about the mystery of Inspiration, which no one can fathom, why should we not simply accept what the Bible says about itself,[1] and then proceed upon the assumption that God is speaking today through the Book? Likewise does he speak through the preacher and the sermon. In each case, the power is from above.

In order to speak effectively from the Bible, the minister needs to know homiletics. Almost every divine who has attained distinction as a biblical preacher has somehow made a special study of this holy art. In the olden time Chrysostom and Augustine came into the ministry after long, careful schooling in rhetoric and oratory. In later years each of them wrote a treatise about the use of these principles in Christian preaching. In later times, unfortunately, Robertson and Mc-Laren did not write or lecture on the art of preaching. But either of them could have done so with distinction. Each of them made a long and loving study of how to preach. Among more recent biblical preachers, here is a partial list of men who have published books about homiletics: William M. Taylor, Charles H. Spurgeon, Joseph Parker, James Stalker, John Henry Jowett, G. Campbell Morgan, Clarence E. Macartney, and George A. Buttrick. At least three of them— Taylor, Stalker, and Macartney—have written about the subject in the form of biographical studies. What have such men to say about the growth of the biblical sermon?

---

[1] E.g., Isa. 55:10, 11; II Tim. 3:15-17; Heb. 1:1, 2a; II Pet. 1:21.

PREACHING FROM THE BIBLE

Whatever else the biblical sermon may have, or not have, it should have structure. The biblical sermon ought to be a popular lesson. A lesson is something to be taught. Hence the minister should plan each message. The introduction should prepare the learner for what is to come; the main body should impress on his mind and heart the chief aspects of the chosen truth; the closing words should send him forth resolved to do the will of God as thus revealed. All of this is as old as the art of preaching. In biblical homiletics there is little that is new. In every such sermon, while substance is the chief concern, structure is likewise essential. Like a house, a teaching sermon stands or falls according to the strength or the weakness of the structure.

In a biblical sermon the most vital part, except the passage itself, is the conclusion. It embodies the practical purpose of the whole discourse. In preparing a sermon, one begins with thoughts about the destination. If one thinks about the inspirational talk as somewhat like a midwinter cruise to the West Indies, where one will stop at various ports and gain fleeting glimpses of many fascinating scenes, one may think of the teaching message as being like a longer journey with a serious purpose. In planning how to make the trip, one begins by thinking about the destination. The end crowns all.

In preparing a sermon a clear vision of the end is a help in deciding about details. A clear sense of purpose guides one in choosing the text. For example, in preaching from Luke 19:1-10, which verse shall one announce—the fifth, the ninth, or the tenth? That depends upon one's purpose. So does the phrasing of the topic. It may be "Jesus in the Home,"

"The Conversion of a Businessman" (really he was a politi-
cian!), or "Jesus and the Individual." From a different point
of view, one may preach about "Why Jesus Came to Earth."
In its turn, the topic influences the phrasing of the few main
headings. Thus the pattern of the sermon throughout should
be like the Master's seamless robe.

For instance, here is a sermon by James Reid, of Eastbourne,
England, who writes the devotional article for almost every
issue of *The British Weekly*. Starting from this paragraph
in Luke, the preacher takes as his subject, "How Christ Wins
His Way." [2] This topic dominates the introduction, the
main sentences, and everything else in the way of structure
or substance. All the materials—except an illustration from
Hawthorne's *Scarlet Letter,* and a few snatches of verse—
come directly from the passage. This man surely knows homiletics! Better still, he knows the Bible. Best of all, he knows
the Lord.

As for the basic plan, there is no rule, unless it be this:
from week to week avoid sameness. As Henry Ward Beecher
used to say, when the sermon starts, no one in church should
be able to guess what he is about to hear; and after the sermon
ends, every one present should know what he has heard.
Such a working principle calls for variety of structure from
week to week. From this point of view, McLaren is scarcely
a model. His sermons tend to be much alike. Three out of
four conform to the traditional type, according to which the
Trinitarian preacher builds a house with three stories. There
is a good deal to be said, however, for occasional sermons of
this traditional type.

---

[2] *The Victory of God,* Hodder & Stoughton, London, 1933, pp. 76-86.

Especially when the time for preaching is short, there is a real advantage in following the custom of F. W. Robertson. As a rule he singled out a text which contains two contrasting ideas. Then he embodied the two ideas in his sermon. For variety he depended upon wisdom in choosing his texts. In quite different fashion Harry Emerson Fosdick often employs the principle of contrast. Some of his sermons are more biblical than others. Whether any particular sermon is strongly biblical or not, it is almost certain to afford an object lesson of structure. His structure is sturdy without being stiff. During any one year he brings forth many different patterns, which will repay thoughtful study.

Within any one part of a biblical sermon, as in the Bible itself, the unit of thought is the paragraph. In making the plan it is good to phrase complete sentences, and then to use a key sentence at the beginning of each paragraph. When one sits down to write the sermon, or when one prepares to preach from an outline which one is to follow only with the mind's eye, all that one need do is to state and explain, discuss and illuminate the truth wrapped up in each successive key sentence. If one knows how to use these sentences aright, and how to keep moving along in a single train of thought, sufficiently charged with feeling, one ought to bring forth a sermon marked by unity and order, movement and climax. Better still, one should preach so as to move the will of the hearer Godward.

Now let us think about the introduction. In preparing a sermon, as in writing a book, one should plan the introduction last. The most interesting way to start the sermon may come to view before one has caught a glimpse of the pattern as a whole, but not until one has seen the basic design can one know whether or not this introduction will be appropriate. Ideally there is only one way to bring a sermon to a close, if it is to reach its destination safely and on time, but there may be a score of good ways to begin. Perhaps this is why one is tempted to have three little introductions before one starts to preach. But it is a safe rule to have only one front porch for any one house. The porch ought to fit the house, not the house the porch.

There is always some one introduction which is better than all the rest. There is only one ideal way to strike the keynote of the sermon. This is what Fosdick usually does in his opening sentence. If not there, he strikes the keynote later in the opening paragraph. Fosdick has much to teach us all about this delicate art of introducing a sermon. Anyone who wishes to follow Fosdick's example should learn to use imagination. Then one will look at the waiting sermon and say to oneself: "How can I get my hearer to think with me about this subject at the very start? How can I lead him to focus his attention on the truth of God which shines out from this passage?"

Let us hear a negative answer:

The most common introduction is usually the poorest; namely, the kind which consists in telling the story of the context, or watering it down in a sea of words. The people generally know the story; probably the preacher has read it to them only a few minutes before, and they should be credited with human intelligence. Of course the context must sometimes be explained, but this should be done briefly, and often it can wisely be let alone. While the preacher is wandering round in his introduction, many a hearer must feel like crying out to him, "Play ball!" Let the sermon start right off the bat!

Every sermon is interesting at the beginning in the sense that the preacher has the attention of the congregation, and if he catches this interest at its first tide, he may hold it and it will lead him on to fortune.[3]

USING SECULAR MATERIAL

A good deal of a biblical preacher's effectiveness depends upon his habit of preaching in terms of today. A vast deal of ineffective biblical sermonizing is almost post mortem. In the study the dry-as-dust preacher might keep humming, "My days among the dead are passed." His mistake is in dealing with biblical facts without taking time to discover what they mean today, and what difference they should make to the layman who must keep his feet on the rock in a time of uncertainty and dread. From John Henry Jowett one should learn how to take a definite portion of Scripture and hold it up so that the sunlight of God will shine through. Jowett preached in New York City throughout the first World War. While he did not say much directly about the war, he kept using the Bible to meet the needs of the man in the pew.

As a study of effective sermons will show, the way to preach with interest is to use facts, facts, facts. Many of the facts come from the Bible, especially from the chosen passage; other facts are from life and thought today. In the modern sense of the terms, there is no first-class popular writing or speaking without the use of concrete facts. "Three-fourths of writing well consists in giving definite, well-chosen facts, and plenty of them; the other fourth doesn't matter." [4]

---

[3] James H. Snowden, *The Psychology of Religion,* Revell, 1916, p. 299.
[4] Reed Smith, *Learning to Write in College,* Little, Brown, 1939, p. 11— a wise, helpful book.

In New York City one Sunday morning a few years ago Charles E. Jefferson was preaching in his former pulpit at the Broadway Tabernacle. He was speaking about the parables in Luke. The purpose evidently was to persuade his hearer to read the parables in Luke, and to do so with the eye of a lover. The method was that of using facts from the parables in order to show how human they are, and likewise how divine. For the grandfather sitting in a front pew, and for the lad of twelve at his side, the sermon caused new light to break forth from the Gospel of Luke. That afternoon when the two of them together read the Third Gospel, they watched eagerly for every parable, and henceforth they looked upon it as a lifelong friend.

In that sermon there were no illustrations, for the same reason that one needs no special illumination in a sun porch on a bright day in December. But in popular preaching, as a rule, there is need for illustrations.[5] In using them one should strive to keep the quality high and the number low. No one of us has ever used too many good illustrations, or too few poor ones. A first-class illustration is like a window which lets the morning sunlight stream into the dining room. A poor illustration is like a sham window which admits no light, and permits no person to look out. A single illustration of this sort is one too many. For a series of object lessons showing how to use various sorts of illustrations, both freely and effectively, consult the recent volume of sermons by James S. Stewart,[6] who is said to be the most popular young preacher now in Edinburgh. Fortunately, the way to learn

---

[5] See Dawson C. Bryan, *The Art of Illustrating Sermons*, Cokesbury, 1938.
[6] *The Gates of New Life*, Scribner, 1940.

to use such illustrations is to keep using them, provided one uses them well. The habit grows.

The biblical sermon is often better in substance than structure, and in structure than style. But it is not so with the written work of ministers as different as John Henry Jowett and George A. Buttrick. Like many others who have been educated abroad, where schoolboys learn how to use the King's English by working with the "dead languages," such a minister cherishes a lofty ideal of preaching as a fine art. By reading one of the poets, and by using his pen, the interpreter cultivates his sense of literary style. He loves to use his pen every day. *"Nulla dies sine linea."* When he has to buy a new pen he may dedicate it to God by a definite act of prayer. Apart from the Bible and the hymnal, that pen is the most important part of his equipment. But the pen is no substitute for brains. As the late Mrs. Einstein told a neighbor who inquired how the scientist liked his new equipment here at Princeton: "All he needs is a pencil and a piece of paper; the equipment is in his head."

The written work of the thoughtful preacher is notable for clearness. Clearness makes it impossible for him to be misunderstood. It is the result of straight thinking, and lots of it. Often, however, one begins to write before one has thought the sermon through to the end. How then can one hope to be clear? When everything about the plan is ready, one should write out the sermon as a whole. One should write fast, scarcely pausing to draw a conscious breath. Otherwise what should be like the Master's seamless robe may be only a "thing of shreds and patches." At least the tone color is likely not to be consistent. Looking at the sermon as a whole, writing it out as a whole, and preaching it as a whole, is all a matter of habit. Why not enjoy this major part of every week's work? What one does well one learns to enjoy, and what one enjoys one is sure to do well.

The written sermon calls for at least one revision. Two would be better. Instead of writing out both the morning and the evening sermon, it is more profitable to write out the first, and then revise it with care. One can preach the other from an extensive outline. Thus one can have the benefit of careful writing, in order to keep from growing loquacious, and the experience of speaking freely, in order to keep from seeming bookish. The trouble about writing much, rather than well, and revising not at all, is that the more one writes the worse one writes, unless one keeps up the sense of style. A good way to test one's style, provided one has a sensitive ear, is to read aloud a passage of real poetry, or rhythmical prose—it may be from the King James Bible—and then read aloud one's own last sermon, to see if the style is worthy or sloppy.

In a revision one pays special heed to the sentences. Is this one clear? Is that detour necessary? As a rule it is easier to be clear in a short sentence than in a long one. But a succession of short sentences would soon seem choppy. They would call attention to their brevity. They would get on the hearer's nerves. Short sentences jar. Much the same line of thought applies to the choice of words. The short, crisp word from the Anglo-Saxon is more likely to be clear than the sesquipedalian transliteration from an ancient language. However, if one used nothing save words of five or six letters, one's speech might sound like the talk of a boy five or six years old. What one says may be simple, but is it anything else? In our biblical preaching there has been far too much "simple simplicity."

The range and the accuracy of a man's vocabulary afford a sure test of his intellectual power. In the community how far up among men of culture does the average biblical preacher rank? Does he stand higher at fifty years of age than he did at thirty? If he writes out one sermon every week, and only one, revising this one with care, he should keep growing in mental power. Such was largely the secret of Jowett's continued growth. He made a lifelong study of words, and he found his highest joy in using them to body forth the glories which shine in the face of the Redeemer. His experience shows that whenever a man's heart is strongly moved, his words tend to flow in a pleasing rhythm. To love holy words and use them well is to be at least a little like the Creator. He is the supreme Lover of Beauty.

> "God wove a web of loveliness,
> Of clouds and stars and birds,
> But made not anything at all
> So beautiful as words." [7]

DELIVERING THE MESSAGE

Under God, the popular effectiveness of the biblical sermon depends on the literary style more than the substance, and on the delivery more than the literary style. This may be fortunate, since it is easier to learn how to speak than to know what

---

[7] Anna H. Branch, *The Shoes That Danced*, Houghton Mifflin Co., 1905, p. 156.

to preach or how to write. If the biblical interpreter wishes to increase his popular effectiveness, and in time perhaps double it, he should learn how to speak. That is what Mc-Laren did in his early days as an inconspicuous pastor. One of his biographers says that in the time of his glory McLaren owed nine-tenths of his popular effectiveness to "the personal electricity" which went out from him to the waiting people. Such a master of English prose could have taken as his own the saying of the Roman officer: "With a great sum obtained I this freedom."[8]

Among the men who have excelled in preaching from the Bible, there has been a wide divergence of opinion about the ideal way to deliver a sermon. At one extreme is the man who memorizes every message, word by word. In his Yale Lectures, William M. Taylor spoke out of his own experience: "Memoriter preaching is the method which has the greatest advantages with the fewest disadvantages. . . . . The memory is like a friend, and loves to be trusted."[9] But Taylor acknowledged that after ten years of memoriter preaching he had to give up this method. His courage failed him. It is wise to adopt a method which one may later have to abandon? If the memoriter preacher once forgets, he is likely to lose his confidence. Without self-confidence of the Christian sort, no man is able to preach with power.

If the peripatetic preacher has only a score of sermons, and if he can deliver each of them often enough to keep it clearly in mind, the memoriter method may be for him the least unsatisfactory. Even so, the peripatetic preacher's pulpit work

---

[8] Acts 22:28a.
[9] *The Ministry of the World,* New York, 1883, p. 150.

is likely to be oratorical rather than biblical. As for the local minister who must deliver two or three sermons a week, the burden of committing them all to memory might become intolerable. Even if it were not, any one message might seem mechanical. Instead of speaking straight from the heart, he might have to grope after the words, and thus speak haltingly. Who wishes to hear a parrot in the pulpit?

At the other extreme is the minister who reads every word from the manuscript. This was the method of Jowett, of Chalmers, and of Canon H. P. Liddon. Before any minister decides to take his manuscript into the pulpit, however, he should be able to leap lightly over three hurdles, each of which is higher than the last.

First, "Can I bring forth week after week a biblical sermon which by its richness of substance is worthy to appear in print?" In twelve months at St. Paul's in London, H. P. Liddon used to produce only twelve sermons. Much the same is now true of Father Fulton J. Sheen, the eloquent radio preacher in the Roman Catholic Hour.

The second hurdle is higher: "Can I write out this sermon with such skill, and revise it with such care, that it will serve the young college student as a model of English prose?" If the extemporaneous speaker should make a faux pas, it might seem to be only a slip; but if the manuscript preacher departs from the ways of correct speech, or if his diction lacks felicity, he may seem to be an ignoramus or a boor. Who among us is always correct and pleasing in his use of written words?

The third hurdle is the highest: "Can I read this literary masterpiece with such consummate art that I shall not seem to be reading, but rather to be speaking straight from my heart?" This was the way that Jowett planned, wrote, and read. Who else can qualify?

Still another method is that of the man whose words are extemporaneous, but whose ideas are carefully prepared. McLaren, for example, committed practically nothing to memory, and read nothing at all from the manuscript. In the study he made ready as carefully as he could, but in the pulpit he used the words which welled up from his heart as it overflowed.

In some of its many forms this way of speaking is probably the most common among biblical preachers. As a rule extemporaneous preaching would be doubly effective if the minister would write out one sermon a week, and revise that one with care. Like McLaren he might commit to memory the opening and the closing sentence or two, with a few other leading sentences. But as for the sermon as a whole, the form of utterance would be as free as the wind.

At its best this sort of delivery is what the average congregation seems to prefer. At its worst extemporaneous preaching is unutterably bad. But if the method has its pitfalls and its perils, so has everything else that is holy and high. "Wherefore let him that thinketh he standeth take heed lest he fall." [10]

Whichever way the biblical preacher makes ready to deliver his sermon, its popular effectiveness, under God, depends much upon his contagious enthusiasm. In the study his heart burns within him, because he is close to the Living Christ. In the pulpit the same heart should burn within him again. So should the heart of the hearer. This is what the fathers knew as unction; they might have called it God.

---

[10] I Cor. 10:12.

Homiletically, the biblical sermon is likely to be worth as much or as little as it costs, in time and thought, in work and prayer. In his study the prophet can build his altar and on it lay the wood. There he can lovingly place his sacrifice; that is, the waiting sermon. All of this he is glad to do as well as he can, but still he knows that the fire must come down from God. Come it will, if he prays before he works, and if he works in the spirit of prayer. Thus without boasting he can exclaim out of a grateful heart: "The Lord God hath given me the tongue of the learned, that I should know how to speak." [11]

---

[11] See Isa. 50:4a; I Kings 18:32-39.

CHAPTER XII

THE INTERPRETER'S IMAGINATION

THE biblical sermon is likely to be weak where it should be strong; that is, in appealing to the imagination. According to a mighty preacher, Horace Bushnell, the Gospel is "a gift to the imagination." [1] According to a much greater preacher, "Eye hath not seen, nor ear heard, neither have entered into the heart of man, the things which God hath prepared for them that love him; but God hath revealed them unto us by his Spirit." [2] In a high sense God is still revealing these holy mysteries through the preaching of the Word. It is the joyous privilege of the man in the pulpit to see the hidden things of God and then show them to the man in the pew, that he too may see. Since the layman who has grown up since the beginning of the present century has been educated more or less imaginatively, he is most likely to respond to the minister who can see what would be hidden from the eyes of the prosaic sermonizer.

Speaking homiletically, what is the imagination? It is the God-given power which enables the minister to see what is hidden from other eyes, and then share his experience with his friend in the pew. For example, think of the spiritual discernment which God bestowed upon Elisha, and through him upon the younger man who was in training for the

---

[1] *Building Eras in Religion,* Scribner, 1910, pp. 249-85.
[2] I Cor. 2:9, 10*a.*

prophetic office. At a critical stage in Hebrew history those two men were caught in the mountains; they seemed to be hopelessly hemmed in by alien horses and chariots. The younger man cried out to the seer, "Alas, my master! how shall we do? And he answered, Fear not, for they that be with us are more than they that be with them. And Elisha prayed, and said, Lord, I pray thee, open his eyes, that he may see. And the Lord opened the eyes of the young man; and he saw: and, behold, the mountain was full of horses and chariots of fire round about Elisha." [3] Would that every man who is preparing to preach might experience such an opening of the eyes! Thus every preacher would become a seer.

The imagination deals with hidden reality. For example, look at Bunyan's *Pilgrim's Progress,* or his other allegory, *The Holy War.* The difference between Bunyan and the wrong sort of allegorical preachers is that he used his imagination for the glory of the God from whom it came, whereas they rely upon that human substitute known as the fancy. If every minister would saturate his soul in those two works of Bunyan, and in his spiritual autobiography, *Grace Abounding,* there would be in the pulpit more use of the imagination than there seems to have been of late. The prose of Bunyan, like that in the King James Bible, is often closely akin to poetry. In poetry, as in lofty prose, the imagination lifts the words of the writer above the sordid things of earth.

> "As the imagination bodies forth
> The forms of things unknown, the poet's pen
> Turns them to shapes, and gives to airy nothing
> A local habitation and a name." [4]

---

[3] II Kings 6:15-17.
[4] Shakespeare, *A Midsummer Night's Dream.*

THE INTERPRETER'S IMAGINATION

In the history of the pulpit everyone who has excelled as a biblical preacher has done so largely through his appeal to the imagination. Doubtless, also, everyone who has failed as a popular preacher has been lacking here. For an example of how to use the imagination in preaching from a difficult passage, turn to F. W. Robertson's sermon, "The Principle of the Spiritual Harvest."[5] In this message he makes telling use of the figure of the harvest. His central teaching is about the judgment of God on the life of a man. Unlike many sermons about judgment, this one voices encouragement as well as warning. "Whatsoever a man soweth, *that* shall be also reap."

For another example take William M. Taylor's sermon, "Christ before Pilate—Pilate before Christ."[6] The introduction is in terms of Munkácsy's picture, "Christ before Pilate." This painting is on display every year during Easter time at Wanamaker's Store in Philadelphia. In the sermon, after leading the friend in the pew to see what is going on between Christ and Pilate, the preacher shows that the typical man today, like the Roman governor, thinks he is sitting in judgment on Christ, whereas the man himself is under the divine searchlight. At Oberammergau in 1930, and again in 1934, some of us saw this truth as never before. None of us who witnessed the Passion Play can ever forget the scene when Christ stood before the judgment seat, while the mob was howling for his blood. Each of us still keeps asking himself, "If I had been in Pilate's place, what should I have done with Christ?"

---

[5] *Sermons*, first series, London, 1889, pp. 205-17; Gal. 6:6-10.
[6] *Contrary Winds*, Doran, 1883, pp. 37-50; Matt. 27:22a.

Thus we see that in hearing a sermon the listener should become a "seer." For example, take a paragraph from a message by Hugh Thompson Kerr, of Shadyside Presbyterian Church, Pittsburgh. He is preaching about "The Church of the New Testament." He has been showing that every Christian is a priest, and that in his hand there should be a sacrifice. "Do you remember what Paul had in his hand? He was writing to the church at Corinth,[7] a church that tried his patience, and almost broke his heart. He is saying that life to him as a Christian is like a Roman triumph. As he writes you can see it all—the aged senators, the oxen garlanded for sacrifice, the priests robed in beautiful garments, the four white horses, the conqueror, the crown, the wreath of victory, the scepter, the victorious generals."

The preacher goes on to describe what one would see if one were there, as one is in spirit. The climax comes when it appears that Paul, the greatest of missionaries and evangelists, thinks of himself as a slave, standing out on the fringe of the crowd, and throwing incense, as a token of his adoration for the triumphant King. That King is Christ.

For another object lesson turn to Clovis G. Chappell. The following paragraph is from the heart of his message about "A Mother's Reward":

In the little Palace Beautiful there are four rooms. The first is a room called Fancy. In this room, looking out towards the South, sleeps a little child, a beautiful baby. It is the Child-That-Never-Was. It is longed for, hoped for, dreamed of, but it never came. In the next room, looking out towards the sunset, the room called Memory, the Child-That-Was. Here sleeps the little fellow that came and stayed just long

---

[7] II Cor. 2:14.

enough to gather up all our hearts before he went away. In the room toward the North, the room of Experience, is the Child-That-Is. He is the little fellow that now plays in your home or is in your Sunday school class. And in the room looking out towards the sunrise, the room called Hope, is the Child-That-Is-to-Be.[8]

In a volume published five years later, the same imaginative quality is prominent. A careful reading of these two books will show how the popular interpreter's powers keep growing if he keeps using them properly every week. In the latter book the sermonic interpretation tends to stand out more clearly, and there is more incentive for the hearer to read the basic passage in the Bible, before he goes out to do the will of God as there revealed. For instance, read the opening paragraph of Chappell's sermon, "My Audience," or "The Four Soils." Note that the appeal is to the sense of sight:

The story of which these words are the climax takes us out into the open country. It is a farm scene. Now I confess that I always feel at home when I get on the farm. I can walk there with a stride of assurance. It is true that this is an oriental rather than an occidental farm, but the picture that it paints is as vivid and familiar to us who had the privilege of growing up in the country as if the Master had lived among us and had, only yesterday, spoken it to ourselves. When I read it, it does not take me across the seas and centuries and continents to distant Palestine; it rather takes me just beyond the hills to the old farm upon which I grew to manhood. Again I am under the blue skies, unstained by a single wisp of smoke. Again I am enjoying the sweet fragrance of the upturned soil. Once more I see the sower sowing the seed, and sometimes the sower is none other than myself.[9]

[8] *Sermons on Biblical Characters*, Doran, 1928, p. 166. Used by permission of Harper & Brothers, publishers.
[9] *Sermons from the Parables*, Cokesbury, 1933, p. 23; Matt. 13:9. Copyright, 1933. Used by permission of Abingdon-Cokesbury Press.

If this is what one means by the imagination, why do many good people fear the use of it in preaching? Perhaps because they confuse imagination with fancy. Fancy tries to get the man in the pew to see what is not real. Unreal "sermonizing" may at times be beautiful, both to ear and eye. The scene conjured up by fancy may be tantalizing. So is a mirage. But it affords the weary pilgrim no water, no food, no rest. By using fancy, the ingenious homilete can make any passage in the Bible seem to mean whatever he wishes. When Bunyan used imagination he made it possible for one to see what lies beyond the bounds of time and space. But when a minister relies upon fancy, he conjures up a picture of what never was on earth or in heaven. The Lord deliver his people from the fanciful preacher!

As an object lesson, take Richard C. Trench's "interpretation" of the Master's tale about what it means to be a good neighbor.[10] In many respects Trench's book on the parables is second to none in English. But he must have been dreaming when he came to the story of the Good Samaritan. Trench says that the traveler is "personified human nature"; the Good Samaritan is the Lord Jesus; the inn is the Church; the two pence may be the sacraments, and so on. If such allegorical substitutes for sweet simplicity went still further, the ass in the story might represent the man in the pulpit. (The reference here is not to Trench!) When the fanciful speaker imagines that he is opening his mouth to make clear the Word of God, he might almost as well be braying at the moon. However, this sort of fanciful preaching has been rare of late. In our prosaic age even fancy seems to have fled. However

---

[10] *Notes on the Parables*, Appleton, 1853, pp. 251-64.

fantastic, fanciful preaching has human interest. But, alas, it lacks divine sanction. It is not so, however, with the most wondrous of man's powers, the imagination.

USING THE IMAGINATION

In preaching, as in any other art, the imagination works on different levels. Let us think of three. We shall begin with the lowest, the descriptive. Here everyone ought to feel at home. At least among ministers, everyone has the descriptive imagination when he is young. If he will feed it with facts, and exercise it daily, so as to keep it strong, he will grow in imaginative power. Thus he can help the man in the pew to see what may have happened far away and long ago. For example, here are chapter headings in a best-seller among secular books of non-fiction: "The Nation Finds Itself," "America Secedes from the Empire," "The Sun Rises in the West," "Brothers' Blood," "America Revisits the Old World." [11] These last two phrases point to our own War of 1861-65 and to our part in the first World War. How will even the ablest descriptive writer put into words the horrors of our present day? Only by seeing what he says!

For better examples of the descriptive imagination, turn to Macaulay's *History of England*. There was a time when scientific students of history made light of Macaulay because he dared to use the imagination. But now the most capable workers in the field of history are coming to see that the heart as well as the head must enter into the interpretation of what happened in other days. Perhaps this is why almost every strong biblical preacher has been an ardent lover of history,

---

[11] James Truslow Adams, *The Epic of America*.

especially in the form of biography. Such a preacher loves to recall the closing words in Macaulay's *History*. Macaulay has been writing about the death of stern King William. "When his remains were laid out, it was found that he wore next to his skin a small piece of black silk riband. The lords in waiting ordered it to be taken off. It contained a gold ring and a lock of Mary's hair." [12]

Largely through reading the words of those who can write, the pulpit expositor learns to employ the descriptive imagination indirectly. Instead of using many words to describe stern King William's devotion to charming Queen Mary, who was a saint, the man with imagination puts his idea into a picture. The intelligent hearer would soon grow weary of word painting for its own sake, but he relishes such a paragraph as this one from Harris E. Kirk. The message is about the God of Jacob, a man who used to be bad. The topic is "Journey's End." To feel the force of the words one should think of the preacher as a visitor from the States. He is standing in the pulpit of a famous church almost beneath the shadow of the king's palace in London. The time is a few years after the end of the first World War, and a few years before the outbreak of another war still more dreadful. At such an hour of tragic memory and fearful waiting, has the man of God any word of assurance and hope?

This strange quickening of hope in old hearts is one of the most beautiful things in life. Lay on the dark colours as you will, still there ever remains some work of noble note yet to be done, some fine flair of enthusiasm and high desire, to temper the asperities of old age. And so it was with Jacob. His story is opening out again; some rare surprises hiding

---

[12] Longmans, London, 1889, II, 773.

THE INTERPRETER'S IMAGINATION

there just beyond the horizon, and waiting for him. He willingly forgot his crooked past. It is time to let the dead bury their dead, and we will go along with him on this long last march to Journey's End, and see this thing that God had kept like a beautiful secret, to reward this life of checkered memories.[13]

Such a preacher sees what he says. He has the descriptive imagination. By using it indirectly, he makes the hearer long to see what lies round the next turn in the pathway towards "Journey's End." Much better than the descriptive imagination is the constructive. This is the synthesizing power. The God of Wisdom bestows this power upon every man whom he calls to put things together in the form of a living sermon. In this same little book by Kirk the closing message is "What God Thought about It." The fourth paragraph appears below. A study of this paragraph, and of the entire message, as well as the other nine sermons, will show how the interpreter puts things together. Thus he enables the man in the pew to look back over his own checkered career and see how God has been leading him all the way. While the man in the pulpit is speaking about Jacob, the man in the pew keeps thinking about himself as a sinner, or rather, about himself in the hands of God. Ere long he should put God first. Says Dr. Kirk:

Let us begin by asking who is the hero of this tale? Here they stand, good men all: Abraham, Isaac, and Jacob, founders in succession of that remarkable race which gave the greatest religion to mankind. There is much in their history that is tragic, wonderful, and illuminating. No one can call the story of Jacob a dull story, neither can we evade its searching application to our own lives. Still, we shall miss its real sig-

---

[13] *A Man of Property*, Harper, 1935, p. 81. Used by permission of Harper & Brothers, publishers.

nificance if we fix upon any one of these men as the real hero of the story. My own reading of the tale, as I have felt the gradual disclosure of its divine significance, has convinced me that God himself is the hero.[14]

On its third and loftiest level, the imagination is creative. This is the realm where only the man of genius makes his abode. Such a man was Bunyan. But it is a realm into which the man with "pulpit talent" can soar from time to time. As an example of a minister who sometimes uses creative imagination, but often does not, take G. Campbell Morgan. In 1913, at a noonday meeting for men in downtown Pittsburgh, he spoke for twenty minutes from the fifty-fifth chapter of Isaiah. Although the time was brief, and the trail was long, the preacher did not seem to be in haste. With a flash here and another there he lighted the trail so that everyone could see whither the guide was leading. The heart of the message was that the man in the pew should get right with God, at once.

In order to make real his chapter as a whole, the man in the pulpit singled out the central verse. To it he kept pointing as to a sort of dividing ridge. He showed that throughout the first six verses there is a crowd of city men who have sold their souls for gold which they failed to get. Among them is hunger and thirst, loss of money and lack of work, a mood of wistfulness and even despair. But as soon as any one in this throng becomes a pilgrim of faith, and thus passes over the dividing ridge where he gets right with God, the scene swiftly changes. For the pilgrim of faith, life now begins to be full of beauty and peace, joy and hope. Such is the seer's interpre-

---

[14] *Ibid.*, p. 99. Used by permission of Harper & Brothers, publishers.

tation of the last six verses in this golden chapter. Here, then, is the pilgrim's progress over the dividing ridge and on into the garden of God!

As a spoken sermon, that was the most memorable utterance which some of us have ever heard. To this very hour, after twenty-six years, the writer can close his eyes and see that dividing ridge. On it he can even descry the Cross, "towering o'er the wrecks of time," as doubtless the Cross still does stand on the mountain top above Oberammergau. Prior to that noonday sermon no one of us had ever seen that dividing ridge where one gets right with God. Now as one repeats the chapter from memory, one can see nothing else so clearly as that dividing ridge, where the pilgrim kneels at the foot of the Cross, to find pardon and peace, hope and joy. Surely such a preacher is a seer.

What is the secret of creative imagination? There are many surmises. At least one of them sounds plausible. According to the *Gestalt* psychology, there comes a sort of illuminating flash, which enables the exceptional man to see order in the midst of chaos, and then shows him how to bring life into things which are inert. In terms of the prophet's vision,[15] the facts and truths which should enter into the body of the sermon lie about one in the study like scattered bones, very many and very dry. At the word of the Lord, through the servant whom he calls to preach, the dry bones come together, bone to his bone. Now the sermon has structure, but still the body is dead. In answer to the prayer of God's servant, the Spirit of God comes into the lifeless form. It breathes, it

---

[15] Ezek. 37:1-10.

moves, it has power to do the will of God on earth as it is done in heaven. Such is the miracle of preaching.

Does one mean that the man of God should bring forth the products of creative thinking two or three times a week? No, that would be asking too much from anyone except a genius. But every man who dares to preach ought to have what Horace Bushnell terms "pulpit talent." [16] The man who has pulpit talent is able to soar once in a while; often he can run without growing weary; sometimes he can only plod along through sand or mud. But if there is in the pulpit any shivering mortal who never soars, or even runs, who must plod along like an ox hitched to the plow, he should ask himself whether or not he has found the task for which God girded him. [17] To every man whom the Lord God has called into the highest and holiest and hardest work in all our world, there should come at times a sense of vision, as from God. The vision will enable him to preach with a power not his own, and with a joy which the world can neither give nor take away.

LIGHTING UP THE SERMON

In the growth of the sermon the imagination ought to guide at every stage. At any one stage this God-given power may be working descriptively, or constructively, or even creatively. Once in a while it may work in all these ways simultaneously. From this point of view let us think of the imagination in three other respects. All the while let us remember that the imagination itself is one; it is the God-given power which

---

[16] *Building Eras,* Scribner, 1910, pp. 182-220.
[17] See Bushnell's famous sermon, "Every Man's Life a Plan of God," *The New Life,* London, 1892, pp. 1-15.

enables the minister to see. Perhaps a better name would be insight.[18] True insight enables the minister to feel at home in the three realms where he should spend most of his waking hours; that is, out in the parish, down in the study, and up in the pulpit. For convenience we shall speak of the three realms as the pastoral, the biblical, and the homiletical. Of course they overlap.

First of all, the minister should have pastoral insight. When he comes into a home which is lying under the shadow of a sudden sorrow, or when he welcomes into his study a friend who has stumbled and fallen into beastly sin, the pastor should be able to see into the depths of the soul, much as the specialist in medicine looks at the heart through the fluoroscope. Pastoral insight enables the minister to diagnose the disease of the soul. Likewise does it enable him to determine what he should preach from Sunday to Sunday.[19] Of course he knows that the needs of men are much the same from age to age. If he were a pedant he might pride himself on preaching eternal truths with no reference to the spiritual ailments now prevailing in the parish. That kind of preacher would probably be a quack. Whatever the malady, he would prescribe a strong dose of physic. But if the family physician followed a similar course, the same parson might pray to be delivered from sudden death.

The physician of the soul is likewise the teacher of the truth as it is in God. As a teacher the minister knows that ignorance today is much the same as of old. Still the teacher ought to know the mind of today, and how to meet its needs. If the

---

[18] Cf. Josiah Royce, *The Sources of Religious Insight,* Scribner, 1912, pp. 5-7, 17.
[19] See *Pastoral Psychiatry,* by John S. Bonnell, Harper, 1938, Chap. IV.

parson lacks a sense of humor, he is likely once in a while to concoct a nauseating mixture. That was the case in a certain rural parish where it was the custom to hold preparatory services on the Saturday afternoon preceding the quarterly celebration of the Sacrament.

At a preparatory service the visiting parson spent forty minutes trying to prove that Paul did not write the Epistle to the Hebrews. Those farmers knew the Bible, and they resented "heresy." So did their wives. Practically every person present knew that the King James Bible ascribes the epistle to Paul. Most incensed of all was the pastor. He could not brook an attack upon the Ark of the Covenant! The next morning, before he invited his friends to commune, he used half an hour trying to prove that even in its editorial additions the King James Bible is both inspired and infallible. Since neither minister was notable for biblical insight or homiletical skill, neither discourse was a masterpiece worthy to appear in print. But even if either had been a piece of controversial prose worthy of John Milton, would that have been the way to prepare weary farmers and their wearier wives for sitting at the heavenly feast with the King of Kings? In other words, each of those ministers lacked pastoral insight, which may sometimes be only another name for plain horse sense.

Pastoral insight goes far to account for the popular appeal of Harry Emerson Fosdick. In some respects he is perhaps the most skillful homilete on this side of the water. Whenever he preaches he strives to use his skill in solving some problem of the man in the pew.[20] Hence the peracher has a

---

[20] Cf. his article, "What Is the Matter with Preaching?" *Harper's Magazine*, July, 1928.

clear sense of purpose and of direction. He seems to be determined to preach what he thinks the hearer needs at the hour. For example, take one of his more biblical sermons, "Forgiveness of Sins." [21] After stating his purpose at the start, Fosdick makes everyone present feel that he is a sinner. Then the preacher brings forth God's remedy for this deadly disease of the soul. Such a sermon is a proof that the man in the pulpit has the insight of the pastor.

In preparing a sermon the minister likewise needs biblical insight. He should use insight constantly during the long quiet morning hours in his study, five days in the week. In the study he needs most of all the ability to see what is in the Book. Strange as it may seem to the novice, he cannot turn automatically to his concordance, his Bible dictionary, and his other books, to find there the passage inspired of God to meet a definite need out in the parish. For example, in July there may be among God's people a mild epidemic of what we Americans call "a fit of the blues," and what the Scotch describe as "being down in the dumps." Where in the books can the parson find the appropriate passage about "dejection," "depression," "despair," "despondency," "discouragement," or "disillusionment"?

It would be easy to waste an hour and likewise fray one's nerves while searching for such a heading among the books known as "helps" and hindrances to preaching power. After a few experiments the weary parson may conclude that he is not called to become a biblical preacher. If so, he may be tempted to resort to cheap American psychology. Psychology of the right sort, whether American or not, has its place in

---

[21] *The Secret of Victorious Living*, Harper, 1934, pp. 110-19.

preaching, as Leslie D. Weatherhead has been making abundantly clear at the City Temple in London. Psychology can help in diagnosis, but only God can cure. As a rule he does so through the Book. In working out the cure he often uses the pastor who has insight.

With the right sort of biblical insight, one should experience no special difficulty in finding a passage inspired of God to meet any crying human need. Rather may one have difficulty in deciding which passage to prefer. In preaching about "God's Cure for the Blues" shall one begin with Elijah's despondency when he sits down under a juniper tree and wishes that he may die? Or shall one start with John the Baptist as he lies in his gloomy prison cell and wonders whether or not Jesus is the Son of God.[22] In either case the message ought to be about God, not about the strong man of middle age who temporarily succumbs to the prevailing disease. For a text which points to God, take the threefold refrain of the forty-second and the forty-third psalm: "Why art thou cast down, O my soul, and why art thou disquieted within me? Hope thou in God, for I shall yet praise him, who is the health of my countenance, and my God." Another topic might be, "The Health of a Good Man's Soul."

Thus far we have assumed that the minister knows his Bible. But what if he does not? Then no degree of insight can take the place of knowledge. Before the imagination can work, in the Bible or in any other field of human thought, there must be something for it to feed upon. No matter how keen the insight, the minister cannot depend upon Mother Hubbard's cupboard to supply him with biblical facts. He

---

[22] I Kings 19:4, 10; Luke 7:19.

must know! Biblical preaching calls for facts, facts, facts. The Bible is full of facts, so full that it is easy to lose one's bearings and fail to find what one seeks. Of course the minister should pray for the guidance of the Holy Spirit, but a few disheartening experiences will show that the Spirit prefers to guide the man who knows how to walk through the many winding pathways in the Book. However, when that guidance comes, it will be largely through what we call the imagination, or insight.

Less important, probably, than pastoral or biblical insight, but still important, is homiletical insight. When one sees the human need waiting to be met, and the passage inspired of God to meet the need, one still must ask, "How can I use this truth to meet that need?" In answering such a practical question week after week, one may adopt the method of John Henry Jowett.[23] In making his sermon plan he used to try out each new part on one hypothetical hearer after another. Each hearer was a real person, who was present only in the mind's eye, though the name may have been down on the work sheet. Almost every week Jowett used to select a small group of the friends who would sit before him on the ensuing Sunday morning—a different group each week—and then use them as a sort of homiletical proving ground.

Equally practical was the method of Joseph R. Sizoo, now at the St. Nicholas Collegiate Church in New York City. When he was at Washington, D. C., his two sons were small, perhaps ten and twelve years. He used to try out on them the coming sermon, before it had begun to assume its finished form— much as grandmother back on the farm used to try out her

---

[23] See *The Preacher, His Life and Work*, Doran, 1912, p. 136.

strawberry preserves on her little fellows. Not every parson has sons of the right age; even if he has, they will soon grow up, and decline to serve as father's sermon-tasters. Nevertheless, every pastor should be forming the priceless habit of keeping before his mind's eye the vision of human faces. As an object lesson of the way in which the method works, here is the opening paragraph in a sermon by Jowett. The text is about abiding in Christ.

There are some people who visit Christ. There are others who abide in him. To the one class, religion is a temporary expedient; to the other, it is a permanent principle. To the one class, Christ is an occasional shelter; to the other, he is an eternal home. By which of the two classes shall we judge the power and ministry of the Christian religion? The evidence afforded by a day-tripper is scarcely sufficient, if we want to know the merits of a health resort, the purity and nimbleness of its air, and the medicinal qualities of its springs. The tripper must give way to the inhabitant; the man who dwells in the sweet, clear air must have the priority over the vagrant whose secret lungs were never bathed in its bracing flood.[24]

A study of these lines, and of the sermon, as well as the book, will show that Jowett had insight of three different sorts, which one labels the pastoral, the biblical, and the homiletical. A thoughtful reading of all his sermons makes one feel that in the popular preaching of a godly man the chief asset is the imagination. While it never takes the place of piety, or of personality, the imagination seems to be the way in which ministerial piety and personality work together for the glory of God and the blessing of man.

A study of this preacher's biography [25] will show that it is

[24] *Apostolic Optimism,* Hodder & Stoughton, London, 1904, pp. 226-28.
[25] *John Henry Jowett,* by Arthur Porritt, Doran, 1924.

possible to keep developing the imagination almost without limit. When Jowett began to preach, he did not seem to be unusually gifted. But by God's blessing upon his ceaseless labors he soon began to be an inspiring pulpit interpreter of the Bible for the common people. His experience shows that the way for the godly pastor to develop this power is to love his people, feed his soul daily on the Book, and work hard on every sermon.

For a far loftier example one turns to John Bunyan's famous word portrait of the man who dwells in the house of the interpreter:

It had eyes lifted up to heaven, the best of books in its hand, the law of truth was written upon its lips, the world was behind its back; it stood as if it pleaded with men, and a crown of gold did hang over its head.[26]

---

[26] *Pilgrim's Progress.*

CHAPTER XIII

THE PRACTICAL ADVANTAGES

AT last we come to the searching question, "Why?" Thus far we have been thinking about what to preach, and how to preach. The answer has been, preach largely from the Bible, and be sure to make your preaching shine! All the while the reader may be wishing to ask: "Why? The preceding chapters have assumed that preaching from the Bible is difficult, especially for the beginner. Such preaching calls for careful study and hard thinking, on the part of a minister who has native ability and technical training. Personally, I am in the habit of working hard. What I wish to know is whether or not preaching from the Bible is worth all the cost."

If the minister knows how to invest his time and energy, he will find that preaching from the Bible produces rich and lasting dividends. As soon as he learns how to make the Bible the basis of his pulpit work, he will find that the benefits are gratifying as well as. cumulative. Some of them have to do primarily with the people. Others chiefly concern the minister. Let us begin with the advantages to the people. They are much more important than the minister. All the while, anything which helps the people is sure to help the pastor, and vice versa. Best of all, whatever helps both people and pastor tends to advance the Kingdom of God.

FOOD FOR THE PEOPLE

The advantages to the people are various. First, this sort of preaching encourages them to read the Bible intelligently. That is what the Christian pastor desires. He wishes that every home in the parish would have its daily altar, that every member of the congregation would have daily private devotions,[1] and that everyone would learn how to enjoy reading the Bible. With such an ideal, the obvious way to promote the use of the Bible among the people is to use it in the pulpit, so that such loving use will become contagious.

In six months, largely through his sermons, any pastor can do much, indirectly, to improve the reading habits of his people. For example, one afternoon at the home of a deacon the young pastor found the daughter reading George Eliot's *Adam Bede*. The young woman laughed as she said, "If I am going to keep up with your preaching, I must become better acquainted with my English classics." In a later parish, after his ideas about preaching had changed, he found that his more thoughtful people were beginning to read missionary biography, such as the life of Mary Slessor, or Christina Forsyth. In each parish the people wanted to become acquainted with the sort of books in which the pastor kept finding his most interesting materials.

In another parish the people have learned to enjoy reading the Bible. The change in their attitude towards the Scriptures began five years ago, when their new minister started feeding them from the Bible. Indirectly he has encouraged them to read other extensive books, such as Margaret Mitchel's *Gone with the Wind,* and Carl Sandburg's four-volume work about Abraham Lincoln, *The War Years.* But this pastor's main

---

[1] See *The Devotional Use of the Bible,* by Peter Green, S.P.C.K., London, 1939.

influence as a lover of good reading has been toward the use
of the Bible as the source-book of the Christian religion. He
has neither exhorted nor scolded. He has simply preached
from the Bible with contagious enthusiasm. His experience
shows that the way to foster a hunger for biblical food is to
keep setting the table with biblical fare.

Second, worthy preaching from the Bible helps to promote
regular attendance at church. Attendance at church is largely
a matter of habit. So is non-attendance. If you ask your lay
friends in this man's parish why they come to church every
Sunday, ahead of time, they will reply: "We are sure to enjoy
an hour of uplifting worship, and a sermon that warms our
souls. Our minister bases everything on the Bible, and he
knows how to make the Bible live." In almost every city of
25,000 or more there is at least one congregation which shows
that the Bible-preaching pastor is the one who has the most
regular church-going people. Of course this kind of pastor
is a good man, who knows how to preach.

Third, preaching from the Bible enables the pastor to supply
the heart needs of his people. "The preacher must live with
the people if he is to know their problems, and he must live
with God if he is to solve them." [2] The obvious way to live
with God all the week is to saturate one's soul in the Book,
and to keep working in the spirit of prayer. Such a minister
devotes long morning hours to his study, chiefly in the Bible,
and five afternoons a week to the pastoral cure of souls. Con-
sequently his sermon from the Bible on next Sunday morning
will be concerned with divine power for human needs among
his own people today.

[2] Joseph Fort Newton, *The New Preaching*, Cokesbury, 1930, p. 41.

218

Fourth, this method of preaching enables the minister to deal publicly with delicate subjects, such as divorce. For example, if there is to be a series about "The Teachings of Jesus for Today," there should be a sermon or two about the home. Much that our Lord says about God and heaven is in terms of the transfigured home. There is in his teachings, also, a good deal about divorce. If the minister is in the habit of preaching from the Bible, tactfully, but without apology or evasion, his people will form the habit of accepting from his lips what the Book says about any subject, however delicate.

Fifth, and most vital of all, preaching from the Bible enables the people to grow in knowledge and in grace. Biblical preaching worthy of the name is teaching. Teaching worthy of the name results in learning. When God's people learn what the Book says about religion and life, they feel a strong desire to do God's holy will. What they do throughout the week should enable the minister to estimate the value of what he says in his sermons. "By their fruits ye shall know them." Where else in the community can one find such radiant characters and such useful servants of mankind as among the people whose minister feeds them from the Book?

GROWTH FOR THE PASTOR

The advantages to the minister are equally practical. First, this sort of preaching requires the minister to master his Bible, as it was written, book by book. In every parish the one man who should be an authority on the Bible is the minister. But to become anything of an authority one needs to spend an hour or more in serious Bible study every day, year after year. The more one learns the more one finds to learn. Amid the distractions of a busy parish, however, it is increasingly difficult to keep up the habit of Bible study, simply for the sake of studying the Bible. But when one knows that every hour spent in such study will some day result in a richer, stronger sermon than one could preach if one did not know a certain book in the Bible, one has a strong incentive for daily toil. Little by little, then more and more, such hours of labor should become sources of delight.

Second, the habit of preaching from the Bible encourages the minister to plan all his work for the pulpit.[3] He looks upon himself as a popular teacher of the Book. Of course he has other duties, but they do not concern us now. As the parish teacher he makes a broad, general plan for the coming year, with a more specific plan for the next quarter—or he may plan by the month—and a still more detailed plan for the coming week. During any one year he plans to work in almost every important field of religious thought, and to deal with almost every important phase of practical duty. Of course he looks at every subject biblically. Thus his pastorate becomes a sort of continuous postgraduate course in biblical interpretation and in practical theology. As he daily watches the growth of the many plants in his homiletical garden, he is tempted to pity any pastor who has never tasted the joys of being a biblical preacher.

Third, this way of preaching tends to keep the pastor at home throughout the week—except during the midsummer vacation—and in his own pulpit every Sunday. A teaching ministry calls for continuous study and for consecutive preach-

---

[3] See *Preaching Week by Week*, by A. Boyd Scott, Hodder & Stoughton, London, 1929.

ing. As soon as he becomes well enough acquainted with the Bible to fall in love with it, the pastor learns to enjoy the long, quiet morning hours in his study, and the high privilege of preaching to his friends every Sunday in his home church. He would rather preach at home than any place else on earth, and the people would rather hear him than any other minister, however brilliant or famous. On the other hand, they feel that if the pastor expects them to come to church every Sunday, he ought to set them a worthy example. If he does so, and if he preaches inspiring sermons from the Book, they will thank God every day for sending them a biblical preacher.

Fourth, this habit of preaching from the Bible prevents needless waste of time and energy in searching for texts and topics. Any adequate way of mastering the Bible, a book at a time, will soon bring out more preaching materials than one is able to use. Any sane, workable plan for using in the pulpit the results of Bible study will enable the minister to bring forth sermon after sermon which will meet the needs of his friends in the parish. Of course no plan will work automatically. Biblical preaching is likely to differ from other ministerial ways of working much as the way of the bee differs from that of the spider. The bee gathers its nectar from garden and field, whereas the spider must spin its tenuous web out of its own inner self. The minister who lives with his Bible day after day, and carefully stores all the sweetness that he gathers, should have in the hive abundance of honey throughout the year. But the minister who must depend upon his own inner impulses from day to day is likely to preach better sermons soon after the summer vacation than at Easter, when he ought to be at his best.

Fifth, and most vital of all, biblical preaching enables the minister to grow, because it requires him to feed his soul daily out of the Book. Since preaching is "truth through personality," it is vitally important that the minister make the most of himself, for the sake of Christ and the Church. "For their sakes I sanctify myself." The way to do that, as the context shows, is "through the truth." [4] Under God, the value of what the minister says from the pulpit depends on what he is at his heart. That in turn depends on how carefully he nurtures his soul. In delivering the charge at the installation of a young pastor, therefore, one might speak from the words of John about "The Health of the Young Minister's Soul": "I wish above all things that thou mayest prosper and be in health, even as thy soul prospereth." [5] If any minister wishes to keep his soul healthy and strong, let him feed it daily from the Book, in the spirit of faith and prayer, carried out in good works.

In *The Christian Century*,[6] Edwin Lewis, professor of theology at Drew Seminary, recently told about his own "discovery of the Bible." In 1924, after he had been teaching in the seminary eight years, he began to prepare for the *Adult Bible Class Monthly* of the Methodist Episcopal Church an exposition of the weekly lesson in the International Series, as well as the critical "Notes on the Text." These services he still continues to render. In 1926 he also became the active editor of *The Abingdon Commentary*. Thus for three years he felt obliged to spend most of his waking hours with the

---

[4] John 17:19*a*.
[5] III John 2.
[6] June 14, 1939, p. 763.

Bible. "Ere long," he writes, "the very Book I was attempting to teach others was itself becoming my effective teacher." The work of expounding the Scriptures in two radically different ways led him to his present custom of looking at all of religion and life from the point of view of the Scriptures. Why should not the pastor, also, make such a personal "discovery of the Bible"?

These facts suggest a line of thought for the charge at the installation of a minister. The subject may be, "The Ideal Minister for Today." The text is about Ezra, whom we should describe as a "teaching minister": "Ezra had prepared his heart to seek the law of the Lord, and to do it, and to teach in Israel statutes and judgments."[7] In the Hebrew the word translated "prepared" literally means to "set," or to fix oneself for action, in the sense of dominant purpose. The verb "to seek" literally means "to search for," as in what we term "exegesis." The ideal minister for today, therefore, is the one who has set his heart upon being a daily student of the Bible, a living example of what it means, and a popular teacher of what it says. According to the commentary by H. E. Ryle,[8] the text points to the disciple seeking for truth, the obedient servant doing what is commanded, the missionary teaching the precepts of God. As the poet sang about the village parson, he was "allured to brighter worlds, and he led the way."[9]

If we glance back now we shall notice that these five advantages are much alike. The substance of them all is that biblical preaching worthy of the name brings the pastor rich

---

[7] Ezra 7:10.
[8] *The Cambridge Bible*, Cambridge University Press, 1891.
[9] Oliver Goldsmith, "The Deserted Village"; cf. the description of the parson in *The Canterbury Tales*, by Geoffrey Chaucer.

rewards, which increase from year to year. The real test in the pulpit will come, however, after he has retired. Will his work stand the test of time? Will he then be able to look back over his years of preaching with satisfaction, or will he have a host of barren regrets? As a rule with scarcely an exception, the aged interpreter who is no longer physically able to serve as a pastor keeps thanking God for having led him into the habit of preaching from the Bible. The aged veteran feels sure that no other way of doing one's pulpit work brings such deep and abiding satisfactions when one must rest in the garden and wait for life's little day on earth to end. "At even there shall be light."

APPENDIX

THE PREACHER'S LIBRARY

THE MINISTER's library is an index of his scholarship, or lack of it. According to the clergymen who visited us from Great Britain and the Continent before the second World War, the average pastor in the United States has a good automobile and a meager library. Even if he has paid the last installment on his car, he may confine his purchases of books largely to homiletical commentaries, volumes of sermons in skeleton form, and various sorts of inspirational froth. If so, what he needs is a plan for the purchase of real books.

SELECTING THE BOOKS

The habit of preaching from the Bible calls for the wise use of books. If the young minister already has on his shelves the regular tools which every man ought to carry with him as he enters his first parish, he ought soon to need more room on his shelves. What, then, should he buy? If the discussion here does not include books on theology, ethics, and other subjects of vital concern, the reason is that we are thinking only about preaching from the Bible. If there are few details about the various works, the reason is that every dealer who handles religious books should be familiar with those listed below. In any case the best source of supply is a man's own denominational publishing house or bookstore.

The basic idea is to purchase a few books at the beginning of every month, and to select these few with care. Since no one of us can advise any other minister about which volumes he will find most helpful, he should form the habit of using a book three or four weeks before he invests. If he earns the reputation of returning borrowed books on time, and of being willing to lend his own, he can have a sort of pastors' exchange library in common with his neighboring brethren. Through the mail, also, he can secure every month five or six meaty books from the library of a theological seminary. Thus in time he can search out and secure the books which will become his lifelong friends. He can also keep his shelves free from second-class stuff. Meanwhile the purpose here is to suggest some of the books which he should try out with a view to possible purchase:

The Bible, Its Origin and Nature, Marcus Dods, 1905.
The Authority of the Bible, C. H. Dodd, 1928.
The English Bible as Literature, Charles A. Dinsmore, 1931.
The Historical Geography of The Holy Land, George Adam Smith, 1931.
Companion to the Bible, Thomas Manson, ed., 1939.
Archaeology and the Bible, George A. Barton, 1938.
The Bible and Archaeology, Sir Frederic Kenyon, 1940.
The Archaeology of Palestine and the Bible, William F. Albright, 1935.
A Brief Biblical History, F. J. Foakes-Jackson, 1930.
How to Enjoy the Bible, Anthony C. Deane, 1925 (for laymen).
The Devotional Use of the Bible, Peter Green (for laymen).
How to Read the Bible, Julian P. Love, 1940.
The Old Testament, Its Making and Meaning, H. W. Robinson, 1937.
Personalities of the Old Testament, Fleming James, 1939.
The Called of God, A. B. Davidson, 1903 (O. T. character studies).
Bible Characters, Alexander Whyte, six volumes, n.d.
The Theology of the Old Testament, A. B. Davidson, 1904.
The Problem of Suffering in the Old Testament, A. S. Peake, 1904.
The Prophets of the Old Testament, A. R. Gordon, 1916.

The Poets of the Old Testament, A. R. Gordon, 1913.
Messianic Prophecy, Charles A. Briggs, 1891.

The books listed thus far deal with the Bible somewhat in general. The pastor likewise needs something specific. For example, in preparing a series on the Ten Commandments he may choose among the books by Robert W. Dale, J. Oswald Dykes, and Henry Sloane Coffin; or else Clovis G. Chappell, *Ten Rules for Living,* sermons, 1938. Among the many writers of popular books about Old Testament characters are George Matheson, W. M. Mackay, Clovis G. Chappell, and Clarence E. Macartney. There is good illustrative material in *The Psalms in Human Life,* by R. E. Prothero, 1909, and in *The Psalms for Every Day,* by Jane T. Stoddart, 1940. The following suggest ways of dealing with difficult subject matter:

Cardinal Ideas of Isaiah, Charles E. Jefferson, 1925.
Cardinal Ideas of Jeremiah, Charles E. Jefferson, 1928.
Prophecy and Religion (a study in Jeremiah), John Skinner, 1922.

The following have to do with the New Testament in general:

Dictionary of Christ and the Gospels, James Hastings, ed., two volumes, 1911.
Dictionary of the Apostolic Church, James Hastings, ed., two volumes, 1916.
The Literature of the New Testament, Ernest F. Scott, 1932.
Christian Beginnings, Morton S. Enslin, 1938.
The Messages of the Books (sermons), F. W. Farrar, 1927.
The Theology of the New Testament, George B. Stevens, 1899.
Studies in the Life of Christ, Andrew M. Fairbairn, 1880.

The Life and Teachings of Jesus, the Christ, A. C. Headlam, 1923.

The Life and Times of Jesus, the Messiah, Alfred Edersheim, two volumes, 1886.

The books listed below deal with aspects of the New Testament. A longer list about the Sermon on the Mount would include the books by Charles Gore, J. Oswald Dykes, and R. L. Ottley; about the Parables, by A. B. Bruce, R. C. Trench, and William M. Taylor (sermons); about the Miracles of Jesus, by R. C. Trench, and William M. Taylor (sermons).

The Heights of Christian Blessedness, Doremus A. Hayes, 1928.

The Heights of Christian Living, Doremus A. Hayes, 1929.

The Heights of Christian Devotion, Doremus A. Hayes, 1930.

The Prayer That Teaches Us to Pray, Marcus Dods, 1889.

Lord, Teach Us to Pray (sermons), Alexander Whyte, n.d.

The Parables of Jesus, George A. Buttrick, 1928.

The Parables of the Kingdom, Charles H. Dodd, 1936.

Understanding the Parables of Our Lord, Albert E. Barnett, 1940.

Sermons from the Miracles, Clovis G. Chappell, 1937.

The Training of the Twelve, A. B. Bruce, 1902.

Pioneers of the Primitive Church, F. V. Filson, 1940.

With the Twelve, Carl A. Glover, 1939.

Epochs in the Life of Peter, A. T. Robertson, 1932.

Peter and His Lord (sermons), C. E. Macartney, 1937.

The Trial and Death of Jesus Christ, James Stalker, 1894.

The Day of the Cross (sermons), William M. Clow, 1910.

The Resurrection Fact, Doremus A. Hayes, 1932.

The small volumes by Charles R. Erdman—one for almost every book in the New Testament—should help the layman to read the Bible devotionally. The following are suggestive for various reasons. Countless others are available.

APPENDIX

The Life and Letters of St. Paul, Conybeare and Howson, 1920.

The Acts of the Apostles in Present-Day Preaching, Halford E. Luccock, two volumes, 1938-39.

The Church in the Roman Empire, Sir William Ramsay, 1911.

St. Paul, the Traveller and the Roman Citizen, Sir William Ramsay, 1901.

Paul's Joy in Christ (Philippians), A. T. Robertson, 1917.

The Redeemed Family of God (Epistles of Peter), J. H. Jowett, n.d.

The Tests of Life (First John), Robert Law, 1914.

The Revelation of Jesus Christ, Donald W. Richardson, 1939.

The Book of Revelation, Ernest F. Scott, 1940.

The Message of the Book of Revelation, Cady H. Allen, 1939.

BUYING COMMENTARIES

More vital than anything thus far in this chapter is the choice of commentaries. In fact, they form the foundation of the biblical preacher's library. At the beginning of his ministry he should form the habit of reading his text or passage in the original language and then consulting a standard commentary or two before he proceeds far in preparing the sermon. For convenience he may have at hand Bishop Gore's *New Commentary,* or *The Abingdon Commentary,* each in a single volume. He may also have a set covering the entire Bible, or at least the New Testament.

Opinions differ widely concerning the merits of various sets. The writer would begin with *The Expositor's Greek Testament.* One reason for beginning here is that any such set encourages a man to use his Greek New Testament every day. No mastery of Greek is necessary in order to use the rapidly increasing series of New Testament commentaries edited by James Moffatt. They are based on his *New Translation,* which is probably the best book of its kind. Anyone who finds these commentaries helpful will also wish to know two books by Halford E. Luccock: *Preaching Values in New Translations of the New Testament* (1928), and *Preaching Values in the Old Testament, in Modern Translations* (1933).

Among the older commentaries which cover the entire Bible, many prefer the set by Lange, as edited by Philip Schaff, in twenty-four volumes. The objection to buying a set is that the volumes are uneven in value. In *The Expositor's Bible,* for example, the volumes by Alexander McLaren, Marcus Dods, George Adam Smith, and a few others, are fruitful. But the treatment of Acts and of certain other books is disappointing. However, the six-volume set is worth all it costs. It takes up little room on one's shelves and is inexpensive to move. Even so, one needs to supplement it with works more directly exegetical.

The part of wisdom seems to be for every preacher to have one or two standard exegetical commentaries on each major book of the Bible. By selecting one book at a time a person is able to judge it on its merits. Here follows a list of separate commentaries which the writer commends for inspection with a view to purchase. Most of them are of the solid type, which calls for study, not mere perusal. No one of them is likely to afford much direct help in homiletics.

GENESIS: Marcus Dods (Expositor's Bible).
    S. R. Driver (Westminster Commentaries).
EXODUS: S. R. Driver (Cambridge Bible).
    A. H. McNeile (Westminster Commentaries).

APPENDIX

LEVITICUS: S. H. Kellogg (Expositor's Bible).

DEUTERONOMY: G. A. Smith (Cambridge Bible).

S. R. Driver (International Critical Commentary).

JOSHUA: G. A. Cooke (Cambridge Bible).

JUDGES: G. A. Cooke (Cambridge Bible).

SAMUEL: A. F. Kirkpatrick (Cambridge Bible).

KINGS: J. R. Lumby (Cambridge Bible).

JOB: A. B. Davidson (Cambridge Bible).

James Strahan, T. & T. Clark, Edinburgh, 1913.

PSALMS: A. F. Kirkpatrick (Cambridge Bible).

Alex. McLaren (Expositor's Bible).

PROVERBS: T. T. Perowne (Cambridge Bible).

R. F. Horton (Expositor's Bible).

ISAIAH: G. A. Smith (Expositor's Bible).

J. Skinner (Cambridge Bible).

JEREMIAH: A. W. Streane (Cambridge Bible).

EZEKIEL: A. B. Davidson (Cambridge Bible).

John Skinner (Expositor's Bible).

DANIEL: S. R. Driver (Cambridge Bible).

C. M. Cobern (Whedon's Commentary).

MINOR PROPHETS: G. A. Smith (Expositor's Bible).

MATTHEW: Alfred Plummer, Scribner, New York and London, 1909.

A. H. McNeile, Macmillan, London, 1915.

MARK: H. B. Swete, 3d ed., Macmillan, London and New York, 1908.

A. E. J. Rawlinson (Westminster Commentaries).

LUKE: Alfred Plummer (International Critical Commentary).

Frédéric Godet, T. & T. Clark, Edinburgh, 1889.

JOHN: B. F. Westcott (Bible Commentary).

A. Plummer (Cambridge Bible).

Marcus Dods (Expositor's Bible).

J. H. Bernard (International Critical Commentary).

ACTS: R. B. Rackham (Westminster Commentaries).

J. R. Lumby (Cambridge Bible).

ROMANS: Wm. Sanday and A. C. Headlam (International Critical Commentary).

H. C. G. Moule (Expositor's Bible).

I CORINTHIANS: Archibald Robertson and Alfred Plummer (International Critical Commentary).

Marcus Dods (Expositor's Bible).

R. St. J. Parry (Cambridge Bible).

II CORINTHIANS: Alfred Plummer (International Critical Commentary).

J. Denney (Expositor's Bible).

GALATIANS: J. B. Lightfoot, Macmillan, London, 1921.

W. M. Ramsay, Putnam, New York, 1900.

Martin Luther, Robert Carter, New York, 1848.

EPHESIANS: B. F. Westcott, Macmillan, London and New York, 1906.

H. C. G. Moule (Cambridge Bible).

PHILIPPIANS: J. B. Lightfoot, Macmillan, London, 1885.

Maurice Jones (Westminster Commentaries).

COLOSSIANS AND PHILEMON: J. B. Lightfoot, Macmillan, London and New York, 1897.

Alex. McLaren (Expositor's Bible).

THESSALONIANS: G. G. Findlay (Cambridge Bible).

PASTORAL EPISTLES: E. F. Brown (Westminster Commentaries).

HEBREWS: B. F. Westcott, Macmillan, London, 1909.

A. B. Davidson, T. & T. Clark, Edinburgh, 1882.

T. C. Edwards (Expositor's Bible).

JAMES: J. B. Mayor, Macmillan, London, 1910.

R. J. Knowling (Westminster Commentaries).

I PETER: E. H. Plumptre (Cambridge Bible).

I JOHN: B. F. Westcott, Macmillan, London and New York, 1905.

A. Plummer (Cambridge Bible).

REVELATION: Wm. Milligan (Expositor's Bible).

H. B. Swete, Macmillan, London, 1907.

J. T. Dean, T. & T. Clark, Edinburgh, 1915.

APPENDIX

USING PUBLISHED SERMONS

Opinions differ sharply concerning the wisdom of a minister's reading sermons. If one is tempted to steal the fruits of other men's labors, one ought to let such books severely alone, partly because the lay hearers also read sermons. But no one questions the wisdom of using sermons as the basis for home study in homiletics.[1] The idea is to concentrate for six months, or even a year, on the sermons of a single preacher. First one reads the standard biography, if there is such a book. Then one reads the treatise on homiletics, if the master preacher has left such a work. The real study begins when one takes up a number of his representative sermons, to analyze each of them with care.

For the introductory course one may begin with Frederick W. Robertson. The biography is in two volumes.[2] The sermons of Robertson come in one volume, in four volumes, or in five. Whatever the form, all of these sermons should be on every minister's shelves. In the study of Robertson's work the emphasis may be upon structure.

Next one may turn to Alexander McLaren. The biography by Miss E. T. McLaren is mediocre. The *Expositions* are worthy of note, but the seventeen volumes would be too many to represent one writer. The first set of six—dealing with Genesis, Isaiah, and Matthew—should prove sufficient. With them should be a few books of his sermons: for example, *The Secret of Power,* and *Sermons Preached in Manchester,* the first series and the second. In this study the emphasis may

---

[1] See *The Principles of Preaching,* by Ozora S. Davis, Chicago, 1929.
[2] *Life and Letters of Fred W. Robertson,* edited by Stopford A. Brooke, 2 vols., London, 1873.

be upon the use of the Bible in preaching, as well as upon structure.

Thus one might go on from year to year, with profit and growing delight. One could take up in turn the sermonic writings of Alexander Whyte, William M. Taylor, William M. Clow, John Henry Jowett, or one's favorite among living preachers. Some of their names appear in the list below. The idea is to select with care the few books which one wishes to study, and then to analyze each sermon as an object lesson of how to use the Bible in meeting the needs of the modern man. This is the sort of intensive work which the minister might do if he secured a leave of absence to engage in graduate work at a theological seminary. But why not study homiletics at home? All that a man of ability needs is a few books, a working method, and a willingness to dig.[3]

Any young minister who wishes to secure a dozen books of sermons, simply for reading, will find these helpful: all of F. W. Robertson; two or three by Phillips Brooks (e.g., *The Candle of the Lord, Sermons for the Church Year,* and *Sermons Preached in English Churches*); three by Horace Bushnell, *Sermons for the New Life, Sermons on Living Subjects,* with *Christ and His Salvation;* three by William M. Clow, *The Cross in Christian Experience, The Secret of the Lord,* and *The Day of the Cross;* with one by James S. Stewart, *The Gates of New Life.*

Among the countless volumes of sermons and sermonic addresses, the ones listed on the following page are worthy of careful reading. The order is alphabetical by authors.

---

[3] For biographical sketches of master preachers see *Princes of the Christian Pulpit and Pastorate,* by Harry C. Howard, 2 vols., Cokesbury, 1927-28.

APPENDIX

Come, Holy Spirit, Barth and Thurneysen, 1933.
God's Search for Man, Barth and Thurneysen, 1935.
Fifth Avenue Sermons, John S. Bonnell, 1936.
Our Faith (not a book of sermons), Emil Brunner, 1936.
God's Turn, Henry Sloane Coffin, 1934.
Christ and Man, Marcus Dods, 1909.
The Healing Cross, H. H. Farmer, 1938.
The Hope of the World, H. E. Fosdick, 1933.
The Secret of Victorious Living, H. E. Fosdick, 1934.
The Power to See It Through, H. E. Fosdick, 1935.
Successful Christian Living, H. E. Fosdick, 1937.
Perspectives, Charles W. Gilkey, 1933.
The Hero in Thy Soul, Arthur J. Gossip, 1929.
The Galilean Accent, A. J. Gossip, 1926.
From the Edge of the Crowd, A. J. Gossip, 1924.
The Living Fountain, Karl Heim, 1936.
The Gospel of the Cross, Karl Heim, 1937.
Let the Church Be the Church, E. G. Homrighausen, 1940.
A Little Book of Sermons, Lynn H. Hough, 1937.
The Christ of the Mount, E. Stanley Jones, 1931.
The Transfigured Christ, John Henry Jowett, 1910.
The Whole Armour of God, John Henry Jowett, 1916.
Crises of the Christ, G. Campbell Morgan, 1903.
The Gateways of the Stars, George H. Morrison, 1931.
The Return of the Angels, George H. Morrison, 1909.
The Angel in the Soul, Joseph Fort Newton, 1934.
The Victory of God, James Reid, 1921.
The Temple in the Heart, James Reid, 1938.
Facing Life with Christ, James Reid, 1940.
The Way of Faith, Joseph R. Sizoo, 1935.
The Forgiveness of Sins, George Adam Smith, 1905.
The Unemployed Carpenter, Ralph W. Sockman, 1935.
Follow Thou Me, George W. Truett, 1935.
With Mercy and with Judgment, Alexander Whyte, n.d.
The Transforming Friendship, Leslie D. Weatherhead, 1933.
The Inescapable God, Leslie D. Weatherhead, 1936.
The Fatal Barter, W. L. Watkinson, 1909.
The Blind Spot, W. L. Watkinson, n.d.

The following books of sermons for boys and girls are well known:

The Children's Year, Walter Russell Bowie, 1916.
The Armour of Youth, Walter Russell Bowie, 1923.
Chimes and the Children, Walter Russell Bowie, 1926.
The Voice Within Us, Stuart Nye Hutchison, 1932.
Holy Ground, Stuart Nye Hutchison, 1934.
Bible Boys and Girls, Stuart Nye Hutchison, 1921.
The Soul of a Child, Stuart Nye Hutchison, 1916.
For the Children's Hour, Stuart Nye Hutchison, 1918.
Children's Gospel Story-Sermons, Hugh Thomson Kerr, 1921.
Children's Worship Story-Sermons, Hugh Thomson Kerr, 1931.
Children's Nature Story-Sermons, Hugh Thomson Kerr, 1923.
Missionary Story-Sermons, Hugh Thomson Kerr, 1915.
Children's Story-Sermons, Hugh Thomson Kerr, 1911.
Children's Everyland Story-Sermons, Hugh Thomson Kerr, 1937.

Thus one might go on indefinitely, for the books in our field are legion. It is the part of wisdom, notwithstanding, to buy one's books a few at a time, and to select these few with care. When the time comes to order by mail the few that one can afford this month, one should look forward with joy to their coming. When they arrive one should set them apart for their holy mission by a definite act of prayer. Day after day as one lives and works among these friends in books' clothing one should keep growing in wisdom and spiritual stature, as well as in favor with God and man. "Other men have labored and ye are entered into their labors." [4]

---

[4] John 4:38.

APPENDIX

What has it all been for? For the knowledge that makes life richer, for the friendship that makes life sweeter, for the training that brings power to the task which is hard and high, for the wisdom that suffers and triumphs and is strong, for the vision that shall light your way like a pillar of fire, for the truth that shall make you free.[5]

---

[5] *Routine and Ideals,* by L. B. R. Briggs, Houghton, Mifflin Co., 1904, p.

INDEX OF PASSAGES FOR PREACHING

INDEX OF PASSAGES FOR PREACHING

INDEX OF SUBJECTS AND PERSONS

245

INDEX OF SUBJECTS AND PERSONS